# GONE TO HELL

## TRUE CRIMES

*of*

## AMERICA'S CLERGY

# GONE TO HELL

## TRUE CRIMES
### *of*
## AMERICA'S CLERGY

RANDALL RADIC

ECW PRESS

Published by ECW Press
2120 Queen Street East, Suite 200, Toronto, Ontario, Canada M4E 1E2
416.694.3348 / info@ecwpress.com

LIBRARY AND ARCHIVES CANADA CATALOGUING IN PUBLICATION

ISBN-13: 978-1-55022-897-7

Radic, Randall
Gone to Hell : true crimes of America's clergy / Randall Radic.

1. Clergy — United States. 2. Crime — United States.
3. Criminals — United States. I. Title.

HV9468.R35A3 2009          364.088´.200973          C2009-902530-2

Cover design: David Gee
Typesetting: Mary Bowness
Printing: Transcontinental   1   2   3   4   5

Though the events related in *Gone to Hell* are based on actual incidents,
some details have been dramatised.

PRINTED AND BOUND IN CANADA

ECW PRESS
ecwpress.com

*For Sharla*

# CONTENTS

# INTRODUCTION

THE WAY THIS BOOK CAME ABOUT was quite peculiar, on the one hand. On the other hand, I guess it could be viewed as a logical development.

It happened this way. On November 4, 2005, I was arrested and placed in a holding cell at the Ripon Police Department. Later I was transported to the San Joaquin County Jail, California, where I was booked, strip-searched, and issued orange jail clothing. Charged with ten felonies, I spent six months in jail. I got out of jail on May 2, 2006.

The only reason I got out was because my attorney cut a deal with the district attorney's office. My part of the deal was pleading guilty to one count of grand theft by embezzlement and agreeing to testify in a murder case. The D.A.'s part of the deal was that I would be released and my sentence reduced to time served.

You might be asking yourself, "Well, what the heck did he do?"

I stole from my church. The technical terms were fraud,

forgery, and embezzlement. But in the end, it came down to stealing.

I was a priest in the Old Catholic Church and the pastor of a church in California. The church owned a house. I lived in the house for free. I mortgaged the house and spent the money on myself. When the money ran out, I sold my church to get more money. Then my crime was discovered by the authorities, everything I owned was seized, my bank accounts were frozen, I was arrested, and I went to jail.

Since I have no intention of boring you with how I did these things — the science of crime, as I call it — I will sum up my brief career as a criminal with one simple sentence. It wasn't worth it.

After I got out of jail, I sat down and wrote about my experiences in jail. Being in jail was like living at the North Pole with farm animals — totally foreign and uncivilized. When I finished the manuscript, I started shopping it around to publishers. One of the publishers, ECW Press, based in Canada, was interested. The guy who ran the company (and still does, by the way) was Jack David. Jack read the manuscript. He liked it. Then he sent me a contract, which I signed, and ECW published the book in April 2009. It was called *A Priest in Hell: Gangs, Murderers, and Snitching in a California Jail.*

I wanted to write another book but wasn't quite sure what to write about. While I tinkered with different ideas, I got an e-mail from Jack. He had an idea. Why didn't I write a book about priests gone bad?

The idea startled me. At first, I was reluctant to do it. I didn't want anyone telling me what to write, you know? That would be like letting someone in my church tell me what to preach about. It just wasn't done.

I thought about it off and on for a few days, letting it percolate in the back of my head. Then I did a little research to find out if it would even be possible. How many priests could be as stupid as I had been? Not many, I told myself. Most of them, I thought, were undoubtedly good, clean-living Christians who would never consider such a thing.

Boy, was I wrong.

Lo and behold! There were lots of them. As I browsed through the news stories, I realized that larcenous priests were a lot more common than I had imagined. Greed was rampant among the clergy.

And what was very interesting was the similarity of what the thieving priests did with the loot after they embezzled it. They bought fancy cars such as Audis and BMWs and Mercedes Benzes and Jaguars. They took expensive vacations and stayed in luxurious resorts in places such as the Bahamas and Bermuda and Europe. They ate at the finest restaurants and drank excellent wines. They furnished their living quarters with upscale furniture. And I mean the good stuff. None of them went to Levitz, that was for sure. And being vain, most of them purchased the best clothes money could buy at exclusive men's shops.

For my part, I drove a BMW 750i. The color was what BMW called "pearlescent black," with a black leather interior. I vacationed at Lake Tahoe and La Jolla. I drank $150 bottles of Opus One wine. I smoked $25 Hoya cigars. And I did something I had always wanted to do but could never afford: I painted. I spent thousands of dollars on oil paints and canvasses and turned the garage at the house I mortgaged into an art studio.

In other words, priests were quite ordinary when it came right down to it. They wanted bling and dazzle like everybody else.

As I read through the stories, I recognized something else. I was small potatoes compared with most of these priests. These guys skimmed millions. And over long periods of time — ten, twenty, even forty years.

Jack's idea was a great idea, I decided. So I wrote this book.

As I wrote each section, a disturbing depression came over me. Like a dark mantle of suffering, it slowly draped itself on me. It was the anguish of sorrow and something more too — the pain of eating the fruit of the tree of the Knowledge of Good and Evil, like Adam did in the Garden of Eden. I knew what was right and what was wrong. And I chose to do wrong. Of course, I regret my choice. But I can't make it go away by saying that I'm full of remorse. I did it. I committed a crime, and crime has consequences. One of the consequences is punishment. The state punished me by sending me to jail. There are other oblique punishments too. Most of my friends are no longer my friends. No one in his or her right mind will hire me as an employee. My reputation is a joke. And the worst punishment is this: I brought all this on myself. I am responsible.

What the priests in this book did was wrong. Wrong in the deepest sense of the word. It was a type of evil, a great wickedness, for they did more than simply steal money: they betrayed the very idea of faith and religion. They ravaged what was holy to human beings — faith, hope, and trust. What they did was a horror, a dread.

I can say that because I did the same thing.

In most of the stories in this book, the priests got off lightly. They got off because of who they were. They were priests, representatives of God and the Church to the people. And because the people hold faith and religion to be holy and sacrosanct, they find it painful and impolite to punish the representatives of holiness. It's as if people can't believe anyone could do what these priests did. It's too foreign, too far-out.

The Church can't believe it either. Embarrassed, it tries to sweep the problem under the rug. If it's out of sight, it's out of mind. That way the Church can go on pretending as if it is perfect and worthy of its charge — the great commission given to it by God.

One problem that comes up over and over again in this book is the latitude the Church gives to its priests, especially regarding finances. Each parish priest functions as his own accountant and treasurer, with total control of the money. Of course, each church has a layperson who carries the title of "treasurer," but in reality this person is nothing more than a clerk who does as instructed. This means there is no oversight and no accountability. The priest is his own little king in his own little kingdom. And as long as he funnels money into the diocesan coffers, no one cares what he does.

A system of checks and balances might resolve the problem but would also wreak cultural havoc on the Church because its modus operandi is based on tradition. If tradition were tossed aside, the Church would never recover, because change is the enemy of Church doctrine. And Church doctrine is based on apostolic succession — the original twelve apostles did it that way, so that's the way we do it. Therefore, change cannot occur. Apostolic succession demands that things be done the same old way.

If you know your New Testament, you know that Judas was the treasurer for the twelve apostles and Jesus. One theory says that Judas was skimming, that's why he turned traitor — to cover up his embezzlement.

Things haven't changed much over the past 2,000 years.

There is probably no solution to the problem. Priests are people, and people are imperfect beings living in an imperfect world. And just how imperfect priests can be is what *Gone to Hell* is all about.

The idea of hell percolates through this book. *Webster's Dictionary* defines hell as "the place where fallen angels, devils, etc. live and to which sinners and unbelievers go after death for torment and eternal punishment." Hell can also be "any place or condition of evil, pain, misery, cruelty, etc." Which brings up the question: is there a real physical place — in the biblical sense — called hell where bad people go after death? Or is hell just a word that connotes human misery and suffering?

As for me, I believe there is a real hell, a lake of fire, where people are punished for their sins. But I probably believe that because that's what I was taught. And when I say, "I believe there is a real hell," that's just an assertion. It's not an argument or a proof.

On the other hand, I have to admit that I have a hard time with a literal, eternal hell where people suffer forever and ever. That seems a little extreme, if you know what I mean. And other super-smart people, a lot smarter than I'll ever dream of being, thought the same thing. They weighed the idea of hell and decided that it wasn't worth a tinker's dam.

The idea of hell is universal. Indeed, the Vikings called their version of eternal torment Niflheim, whose location was given as being in the Far North, beneath the roots of Yggdrasil, the "Tree of the World." The Vikings even went so far as to identify a counterpart to the Christian Great Gulf Fixed; theirs was called the great void Ginnungagap. The Viking heaven was, of course, Valhalla. Entrance into Niflheim was across the

Gjallarbru, "the Echoing Bridge." And, interestingly, the Christian Armageddon is rivaled in the Norse equivalent — Ragnarok, the final battle of the gods and giants.

Hindu, Buddhist, and Zoroastrian hells exist too. However, in each instance, cycles of incarnation can result in advancement out of hell. And the Roman Catholic concept of purgatory found its likeness, according to some, in the Hebrew Abraham's bosom. This was, supposedly, a state of limbo. Others, though, equated it with refrigerium, "the place of refreshment."

In all these instances, purgatory, or its like, was the place where behavior modification took place, a kind of halfway house between heaven and hell. Once modification took place, paradise, or its like, might be achieved. Even Joseph Campbell, the great high priest of modern mythology, has stated that each one must thus enter "the belly of the beast" before achieving heaven.

Satan's wonderfully original statement, "ye shall be as gods," lives on. Humankind still believes that we, by means of good works and constant trying, might achieve our own salvation. If we do, we get to go to heaven. If we don't, we are cast into hell, whatever it might be.

Perhaps hell is simply this: in the idea, and all its variations, humankind senses a tragic finality. So all of humankind strives incessantly to be better and more deserving, assuming that then we might be acceptable to other human beings, to the world in general. Goodness or morality, as a consequence, in one form or another, even if only spiritual, becomes the goal of all.

All that being said, the stories in this book — for the most part — are very entertaining. Almost like a religious version of *One Flew over the Cuckoo's Nest*, where it's a toss-up as to who is the most insane — the priests, the Church, the legal system, or the media. I say for the most part because the story of Father Gerald Robinson is plain old eerie and abnormal and ghastly. In the other stories, though, the sheer audacity of the priests boggles the mind. I mean how — in the name of God — did Father Jacobs, Monsignor Colagiovanni, and Martin Frankel ever think they could get away with what they were doing? Yet they did, for a while anyway. And the reason they did was because no sensible person would suspect anyone of such superabundant gall, especially priests who were supposed to be so meek and mild and harmless.

*Gone to Hell* is about Roman Catholic priests, which might lead readers to think that I dislike the Church or that Catholic priests are worse than the clergy of other religions. That is wrong. I have the greatest respect for the Catholic Church. Which is why I chose to take holy orders in the Old Catholic Church. This book is not about the Roman Catholic Church. It is about priests who chose to become criminals. There are just as many, if not more, clergy of other denominations who crashed and burned. Perhaps I will have the opportunity to write about them in another book.

Priests in business either fool people or get fooled.
— *Cardinal Francis Spellman*

# CHAPTER 1

## MAKING BANK

IN THE "OLD PART" OF TOWN, the St. Vincent Ferrer Catholic Church slumbered beneath the shade of tall palm trees. Built in what some people called the "quasi-modern-Spanish" style, the sprawling buildings had red slate roofs and walls of white stucco. A megachurch, St. Vincent Ferrer boasted over 4,000 members. Most of them grew up attending the church.

In between what used to be called the Florida East Coast Canal (now known as the Intracoastal Waterway) and the Atlantic Ocean sat the city of Delray Beach. About 75,000 lucky people lived there in 2003. It was a clean, pretty city that hosted international tennis tournaments. Lots of rich and famous people strolled around, spending oodles of cash in assorted boutique shops and in upscale restaurants. Quite simply, Delray Beach was a very affluent community.

For forty years, Monsignor John Skehan had looked after the spiritual needs of the parishioners. Very popular, Skehan was a tall, heavyset man who had been born in Dublin, Ireland. His hair was white with age now, but it had once been red. And he peered out at the world with striking blue eyes. Everyone called him "Father John."

As Father John entered the church office in June 2003, Colleen Head could tell something was wrong. Colleen was not only his secretary — one of many employed by the church — but also his close personal friend. She could read his face and always knew when he was upset.

"Good morning, Father John," she said, glancing at the clock on the wall. Ten o'clock. Father John never showed up before ten.

"Morning, Colleen," said the priest as he walked by her desk on his way to his private office.

As she later revealed when interviewed, Colleen stared at his back, wanting to ask him what was the matter. But she knew better. When he felt like talking, he would.

Father John had his hand on the doorknob, then hesitated. Turning around, he looked at Colleen. His Bahama blue eyes, usually sparkling with joy, seemed sad. "Colleen," he said, "do me a favor, would you?"

She nodded. "Of course."

"Come into my office," said the priest. "I need your help with something."

Colleen rose and followed him into the private office. She closed the door behind her and stood waiting.

Father John sat down behind a huge teak desk. He sighed majestically. Leaning back in his chair, he folded his hands together and, with his elbows on the arms of the chair, rested his chin on his hands.

"You know how I like to collect coins, right?" he said.

"Of course."

Everyone knew about his coin addiction, as Colleen called it. The proper term for it was numismatics. But his interest went way beyond studying and collecting coins. It was just like a chemical dependency. She suspected that Father John had other addictions too. But she tried not to think about them. And, besides, they might just be rumors.

"Well," said the priest, "I purchased some rare coins yesterday from a dealer down in Texas. I put them on my American Express card like I always do." He stopped and gazed out the window.

After thirty seconds, Colleen said, "I don't see that that's a problem."

Giving a little start, Father John came back from wherever he had been. "It's not," he said. "The problem is the amount. I didn't realize how much the coins all added up to. I was excited, you see." He gave her a sheepish smile.

"How much were they?" she asked.

"$275,000," he said, rolling his eyes at her.

"Oh, my," gasped Colleen. She moved to one of the leather chairs in front of the desk.

"Yeah," said Father John, chuckling, "'oh, my' about covers it."

"What can you do?" Colleen said, one of her hands touching her throat.

The priest shrugged. "Send some of them back, I guess," he said. "When they arrive, I'll just have to ship them right back to Texas."

"Well, can you do that?"

"I think so," he said. "That's where I was going to ask you to help." He leaned forward and put his elbows on the desk. "Could you call the dealer for me? And tell them I made a mistake — and ask them if I can return some of them?"

"Of course," she said. "I'd be happy to."

He pushed a piece of paper across the desk. "Here's the phone number and my credit card number, in case you need it."

Colleen crossed to the desk and picked up the paper. "First Fidelity Reserve" was written on it in Father John's small script. There was a phone number below it, and below that was another, much longer, number.

"I'll go call right now," said Colleen. "Do you want me to see if they'll let you send it all back?"

"Oh, no," said Father John. "Just $50 to $100,000 worth. My budget only allows $200,000 for coins right now." He flashed Colleen a shy grin. His blue eyes twinkled impishly at his mistake, as if he was a little boy caught with his hand in the cookie jar. "Which is why I'm in this pretty pickle. I simply forgot about my budget."

"Okay," said Colleen. "I'll see what I can do."

"Thanks, Colleen. I really appreciate you and your people skills."

As she shut his office door behind her, Colleen leaned back against the dark wood. Her eyes were wide open and her mouth agape, as if she was watching a horror movie. Nerve endings tingled and squirmed all over her body. She realized she was holding her breath and exhaled.

She couldn't believe it. $275,000! On coins? How could a man — a priest — who made $1,889 a month afford such an amount? Even if he had saved every dime he made for the past ten years, he couldn't. Where did a priest get that kind of money? she wondered as she walked to her desk.

She thought she knew.

There had been many rumors over the years about Father

John and his gambling junkets, about his extravagant vacations, and . . . well . . . even about his girlfriend. Everyone expected a priest to drink a little, especially an Irish priest. People accepted that and didn't condemn it. But this!

And now all this money. It was like pulling down the church's white flag and hoisting in its place a black flag with skull and crossbones on it. Father John was stealing money from his own church. Colleen knew it. She could feel it in her bones. She had to tell someone, so she shared her suspicions with her mother, who later told investigators.

At her desk, Colleen pulled up Word on her computer and wrote an anonymous letter to the Florida attorney general's office. She poured out all her suspicions about what was really going on. She urged the attorney general to investigate. Then she printed it up and proofread it. As she read it, she was struck by how foolish and malicious the letter sounded. She sounded like a jealous wife seeking revenge on a straying husband. The letter reeked of sour grapes: he has all this money, and I don't, so I want to grind him into the dust beneath my chariot wheels. There was no way she could mail this, especially unsigned. Colleen stared at the letter for a few seconds, then made her decision.

Opening the bottom file drawer of her desk, she put the letter in the very back, behind a folder. She could always change her mind later, she told herself. But right now she just couldn't do it. It felt dirty. Besides, she had no real evidence. Just a feeling. And that was not proof.

Colleen shut the file drawer and picked up the phone, dialing the number of First Fidelity Reserve in Beaumont, Texas. Two years later, in June 2005, Colleen would take the letter out of the drawer and mail it. Then all hell would break loose.

But back in August 2003, Father John Skehan was retiring. He'd served God, the Holy Mother Church, the Virgin Mary, and the pope for forty-two years. It was time to enjoy the years that were left to him. He was seventy-six years old. Mostly, he wanted to travel, drink twenty-five-year-old Irish whiskey, and do nothing. He had planned for his retirement forty years ago and had been working and saving and preparing for it ever since. It was time.

Bishop Barbarito, who headed the Diocese of Palm Beach, had selected and appointed Father Skehan's successor. Father John would be replaced by Father Francis Benedict Guinan. Father Francis was sixty years old and was the parish priest at St. Patrick's Catholic Church in nearby Palm Beach Gardens. A suburb of the city of Palm Beach, Palm Beach Gardens was an older, poorer version of Delray Beach. And like an ugly stepsister, Palm Beach Gardens was jealous of Delray's money, status, and fancy tennis tournaments.

Born in County Offaly, Ireland, Francis "Frank" Guinan grew up poor and tough, determined to get ahead in the world. He received his theological education at All Hallows College in Dublin. He became known officially as Father Francis Guinan in 1966, the year he took holy orders. After that, he moved from parish to parish as the bishops told him to. His appointment as the priest at St. Vincent Ferrer Catholic Church would be the pinnacle of his career, what every priest wished for: a wealthy megachurch.

Father Frank and Father John knew each other well. They were both Irishmen, born and raised in the old country. Both were rough-and-tumble kind of guys, physically powerful men. They were both smart. And both were opportunists.

Sitting in Father John's private office, Father Frank

already felt at home. He liked the dark wood paneling and the big teak desk. Gazing out the windows of the office, he approved of the view too. Tall palm trees rustled in the breeze. Manicured green lawns flowed smoothly to the west, where just a strip of blue Atlantic Ocean could be seen. He decided that once he moved in he'd leave the windows open so he could hear the distant crash of the surf.

Father John handed his replacement a tumbler of ice floating in amber whiskey. They touched tumblers with a small clink and took a big swallow.

"Ahhh," said Father John. "The nectar of the gods."

Guinan nodded and smiled. "That it is."

Father John sat back in his chair, resting his tumbler on the shelf of his belly, which plumped out his black clergy shirt. He was proud of his belly. Lots of good food, good whiskey, fine wines, and time had gone into its making. A belly like that didn't grow overnight. He gave it a vain pat.

"Tell me about the church," said Guinan, taking another sip. "Anything vital I need to know?"

Father John shrugged. "No, not really. Same old thing," he said. "Lots of rich people who like to complain." He dropped his chin in confidence. "You'll have to hold lots of hands."

Guinan laughed. "Don't I know it."

"But there is scope," Father John said, gazing intently at his replacement. "An industrious man can do well here."

Guinan finished off his drink and set the tumbler on the desk. He knew he was about to learn Father John Skehan's secret to success.

As Father John poured more of the amber liquid into it, he said, "A capable man can prepare for other things in life . . . and for the expenditures those other things engender."

Father John spoke openly because he'd heard about Guinan through the grapevine. He knew that Guinan was ambitious and unafraid to take a risk. He also knew that Guinan liked to drink. Father John knew other things too. Guinan played twenty-one in Vegas and the horses in Miami, and he had purchased a piece of property in Juno Beach for $154,000. He vacationed in the Bahamas, staying at the lavish and expensive Royal Nassau Hotel, a favorite of movie stars and rock stars. Lastly, Guinan had a girlfriend, a young one who, according to rumor, kept him very busy in the bedroom. In other words, Father John trusted Guinan. They operated in the same manner.

Guinan bared a predatory smile. "Go on," he said, nodding slowly.

"We," said Father John, using a beefy index finger to indicate first Guinan, then himself, "make $1,800 a month."

"One thousand eight hundred and eighty-nine, to be precise," corrected Guinan with an ugly grin.

"Whatever," said Father John. "It's not much, that's for sure. Especially when you consider all the wealthy dolts we endure day after day, week after week, year after year. Hell, I've been here for forty-two years and never once had a raise or a bonus." Bitterness smeared his words and his face.

Guinan nodded his agreement, his mouth a grim line.

"So, what to do?" said Father John, switching to a reasonable voice. He leaned forward. As he did, a black energy clouded his face. "We take what we need," he hissed. "What we deserve. What is rightfully ours." Leaning back, he took another gulp of whiskey.

Guinan's half-closed eyes signaled his approval. "Damn right, we do," he said.

Father John cocked his head to the side and gave Guinan

a level look. "I have," he said, shifting his bulk in his chair. "And I know you have too."

Guinan didn't move. He didn't mind Skehan knowing, he just felt uneasy owning up to it. If he didn't actually say the words, then it was like it never happened.

"This church — St. Vincent's — is the goose that laid the golden egg," said Father John, warming to his subject. "Lots of cash on Sundays, which is immediately taken care of. Lots of checks, which are easily diverted. But they take a little more time and planning."

"How do you 'take care' of the cash?" asked Guinan. This was getting interesting.

"I have my people bundle it up in thousand-dollar stacks. For easier handling," Father John chuckled. "Then later, when no one's around, I remove the ceiling panels and tuck it away topside."

Guinan glanced up. "You mean . . . ?"

"Yeah," drawled Father John, grinning hugely. Then he looked up too. "There's over $300,000 in cash up there even as we speak."

Guinan laughed, shaking his head. "You naughty, naughty boy."

Father John winked roguishly. "That's just the tip of the iceberg," he said. "I've got over half a million in rare coins. A penthouse on Singer Island worth $455,000. Another here in Delray Beach, worth a little more than half a mill. There's a tidy, white cottage in a nice suburb in Dublin, along with a brisk pub. The pub alone nets me $250,000 a year."

As he spoke, Father John rubbed his hand over the rounded edge of his teak desk. The smoothness of the wood pleased him, while the motion calmed him. "And I'm thinking of buying a nice fishing boat," he added. "A fifty-foot

Bertram."

"Whew," breathed Guinan in appreciation. "I'll bet you're sorry to be going, huh?"

"Nah," said Father John, then tossed back his drink. "It's time to enjoy the spoils. While I still have my health. Besides, I've got plenty."

He poured himself another drink and topped off Guinan's glass.

"I don't want to get greedy," he said in a flat voice. After a moment, he let loose a braying laugh, like an old Irish mule who just heard the punch line.

Guinan laughed until his eyes wept. Then he said, "What about the checks? How do you handle those?"

"I've got three slush funds," said Father John, shrugging. "I deposit most of the checks in the church's account. The rest I drop into the slush accounts. Easy."

"Yeah, sounds like," said Guinan. He thought for a second, then said, "How much does the church take in per year — on average?"

"Anywhere between $6 and $10 million," said Father John. "So it's easy for modest amounts to get lost." He grinned and winked again.

"I like it," said Guinan. He glanced around the office, his eyes embracing the walls. "I think I'm really going to like it here."

"I'm sure you will," nodded Father John.

Each Roman Catholic diocese in the United States is self-governing. The bishop in each diocese is like the king of his own little kingdom. No one tells the king what to do. So each bishop sets up his own policies in his diocese. Policies vary as much as people do.

The Diocese of Palm Beach performed audits of its parish churches only when there was a change of pastors. When a priest left or retired and was replaced by a new priest, the diocesan accountant would show up and look at the books. St. Vincent Ferrer Catholic Church had not changed pastors in forty-two years. Which meant the financial books had not been examined in forty-two years.

In September 2003, Father Skehan officially retired. Father Guinan took over as the pastor of St. Vincent Ferrer. According to policy, the books would now be examined.

Denis Hamel parked his car under a group of palm trees. Even though it was September, it was Florida, which meant it was still hot outside. Denis hoped the shade from the trees would keep the black leather interior of his car relatively cool.

As he strolled across the parking lot, the black tarmac seemed to move under his feet. That's how hot it was. Then he remembered he hadn't locked his car. Hesitating, he glanced around, shrugged, and laughed at himself. It's a church, he thought. If it's not safe from crime here, it's not safe anywhere.

Denis, the accountant for the Diocese of Palm Beach, didn't look like an accountant. He didn't wear glasses or have a plastic pocket protector in his white cotton shirt. And the word *nerd* had never been used to describe him. However, the word *suave* was frequently applied to Denis. He looked and dressed like a model on the cover of *GQ* magazine.

Nevertheless, he was a bean counter, and he was here to count the beans of St. Vincent Ferrer. Its books hadn't been seen in over forty years, which meant Denis wasn't even alive the last time an audit was done. Since it was a megachurch, and since most of its members were rich, it would be interesting to see just how much money St. Vincent's had. And what the church was doing with it.

Entering the church's office area, Denis noted four secretaries seated at desks, working at their computers. All of them were middle-aged. A waist-high counter separated the waiting area from the work area. Denis approached the counter.

The woman nearest him looked up and smiled. "Hi," she said. "Welcome to St. Vincent's. How may I help you?"

"My name is Denis Hamel, and I believe I'm expected," he said. "I'm with the Palm Beach diocese. Bishop Barbarito has asked me to confer with Father Guinan regarding St. Vincent's financial statements."

"We were told you were coming," said the woman.

Another of the secretaries rose and walked to the counter. Very pretty in a tense way, with light brown hair, she wore a yellow dress that bleached her skin coloring. "May I help you?" she asked.

"Yes, thank you," said Denis. "My name is Denis Hamel, and I —"

"I heard you," she said.

"Yes. So you did," said Denis. Not a very pleasant woman, he thought to himself.

"Father Guinan is extremely busy at the moment," she said. "I'm sure he doesn't have time for this." She started to turn away. "But I'll check."

She walked back to a door that had IVA on it in gold letters. Knocking, she entered. Before she closed the door, Denis could make out a black-clad figure with a white clerical collar.

Denis waited, feeling the glances of the three remaining women. He definitely felt unpopular, like Frankenstein's monster at a debutante ball.

The door to the private office opened. Out marched the woman in yellow, followed by a tall, rugged-looking priest. The priest frowned at him.

"This is Mr. Hamel," said the woman in yellow, flopping her hand out in a faultfinding gesture.

"I'm Father Guinan," said the priest.

They shook hands. Then Denis explained why he was there.

"I really don't have time for this," said Father Guinan. "Maybe you can make an appointment and come back in a few months."

Denis looked around. "Perhaps we could discuss this in your office," he suggested.

"No," growled the priest. "I told you. I don't have time for this."

"Bishop Barbarito —"

"Can't you hear?" said Father Guinan. "I don't have time right now. Beat it."

Denis took half a step back. "What?"

"I said, beat it."

Then Father Guinan turned and walked back into his office, shutting the door behind him.

The woman in yellow glared at Denis. Her body language was that of an overprotective mother bear.

Denis cleared his throat and beat it. As he walked back to his car, he fumed. The arrogance of the priest was staggering and unacceptable. In fact, his whole attitude was deplorable. Who did this Father Francis Guinan think he was? The bishop himself had sent Denis to begin auditing the books. We'll just see about this, Denis thought as he started his car.

Bishop Gerald Barbarito did not want to hear what he was hearing. That the priest — Father Guinan — of the largest and most affluent church in the diocese had told the diocesan accountant to "beat it." He thought about it for a second and almost laughed out loud. It wasn't funny, of course, but at the same time it really was.

"I should have pressed him," said Denis, standing rigid with anger in the bishop's office. "I should have forced the issue. But when it came right down to it — I didn't really have anything to threaten him with. I mean what was I supposed to say? I'll tell the bishop if you don't cooperate?" Denis rolled his eyes as he remembered the priest's arrogance, telling him to "beat it." Just thinking about it sent his blood boiling.

Bishop Barbarito bit his lip to keep from smiling. It really was humorous, he decided. "No, Denis," said the bishop in an easygoing tone. "You did the correct thing. You handled a potentially volatile situation with tact and tolerance. And I am grateful to you for not — as you put it — pressing him."

Denis gave the bishop a small nod of thanks.

"Perhaps Father Guinan misunderstood your presence. As you know, we try to provide our priests with as much autonomy as possible," said the bishop. "Perhaps he interpreted your presence in a negative way. As if he thought we were implying his bookkeeping might be deficient." Bishop Barbarito paused to think about his own words. A startled look surfaced on his face. "Or worse," he said in a surprised tone. "I mean he may even think that we think he is guilty of some financial indiscretion." He shook his head and glanced at Denis. "I certainly hope he doesn't think that. If he did . . . well, that would explain his reaction."

"Yes, I guess it would," said Denis.

"In any event, I will discuss the matter with Father Guinan. I'm sure it's just a simple misunderstanding. Most things are, you know. Especially around here," said Bishop Barbarito.

The bishop had taken over the Palm Beach diocese at almost the same time Father Guinan had replaced Father Skehan. Barbarito's predecessor had left under a cloud of sexual abuse allegations. Actually, the two previous bishops had been removed from the path of a tornado of scandal just before it hit. Nothing had been proven yet. But the lawsuits were piling up, and Bishop Barbarito felt as if he was running a law firm instead of a diocese. The diocese was ready to collapse because the foundation was rotten.

Bishop Barbarito's primary talent was healing spiritual diseases, getting people to forgive and move forward. That's why Barbarito had been appointed. His job was to repair the spiritual building. And the Palm Beach diocese proved to be a challenge. It was still reeling. The last thing he needed was for his biggest church and its priest to feel insulted.

Accordingly, Bishop Barbarito asked his secretary to phone St. Vincent Ferrer Church and speak with Father Guinan's secretary. His hope was that the two secretaries would check their respective calendars and set up an appointment between him and Father Guinan.

"So that," Bishop Barbarito told his secretary, "Father Guinan and I might discuss diocesan policy regarding periodic, routine audits. So that everyone is on the same page."

Father Guinan's secretary told Bishop Barbarito's secretary that Father Guinan was "unavailable." No reason was given. He was just plain old "unavailable."

Father Guinan's unavailability extended to the next day, then the next, then the next. In fact, it appeared that Father

Guinan would be unavailable — forever.

After a month of this cat-and-mouse game, Bishop Barbarito dictated a letter to his secretary that *ordered* Father Guinan to cooperate with Denis Hamel. All financial records were to be made available to him within a reasonable amount of time — not to exceed five days for each request.

Father Guinan stalled for time. Finally, though, he gave Hamel the financial records for St. Vincent Ferrer Catholic Church — forty-two years of records. It took Hamel and his auditing team almost two full years to work their way through the books.

In April 2005 — just before Good Friday and Easter — Denis sat in his office. He couldn't believe it. "Dumbfounded" described the way he felt. Reaching for his phone, he called Bishop Barbarito.

"Hello," said Barbarito.

"Bishop," said Denis, "Denis Hamel here."

"Denis, how are you?"

"Not so good right now, Your Grace," said Denis.

"I'm sorry to hear that," said Barbarito, concern deepening his voice.

"It's about St. Vincent Ferrer," said Denis. "Actually, about their books."

"Oh." Then silence.

"Your Grace," said Denis slowly, "we have a tiger by the tail."

"Exactly how would you define a tiger by the tail, Denis?" asked the bishop.

Denis sat forward in his chair, picking up a computer printout from his desktop: "$8,600,000 are unaccounted for, Your Grace. That's my definition of a tiger by the tail."

For ten seconds, the bishop said nothing. Finally, Bishop Barbarito cleared his throat. "Perhaps we should meet immediately, Denis," he said.

"I think so, Your Grace," agreed Denis. "I'll be right over."

In most Catholic parishes, the pastors had, and still have, an arrogant and possessive attitude toward the money given to their churches — as if the money in the collection basket belonged to them personally. Worsening the problem of arrogance was the problem of vows. Parish priests did not take a vow of poverty. They did promise to remain celibate. Most priests saw the sacrifice of sex as something they should be repaid for. The surrender of sex authorized them to take more. They were owed something. And that something was money. F. Tupper Saussy discussed this sense of entitlement in his book *Rulers of Evil*, which dragged the Church and its priests over red-hot coals.

Especially in the wealthier churches, the priests resented the splashy cars, the glamorous clothes, and the big houses of their parishioners. Were the two Irish priests envious? Probably. Father Guinan and Father Skehan both grew up dirt poor in Ireland. As pastors, they didn't even make $2,000 a month. Yet most of their parishioners made $100,000 or more per year. The two priests lusted for that which they saw every day — money and the things it could buy.

So did a lot of other priests. According to a Villanova University study of accounting problems in Catholic parishes in the United States, 85% of the parishes reported embezzlement. And 11% of the embezzlement was over $500,000. This meant that 85% of the priests in the Roman Catholic churches were helping themselves to what they thought they deserved — money. The Catholic Church looked more like a crooked casino. Most priests were making sure they got a cut of the profits.

Denis Hamel sat in the bishop's office, which was small and modest compared to those of most bishops.

Bishop Barbarito looked pale. "Tell me," he said.

"Well," said Denis, "all the details aren't certain yet. But so far the total of missing money is — as I said on the phone — $8.6 million. In the past two years, Father Guinan has pilfered in the neighborhood of $645,000 from St. Vincent's."

Bishop Barbarito stifled a groan and shut his eyes, as if by doing so he could make the problem go away. Opening his eyes, he flicked his fingers at Denis. "Go on," said the bishop.

"He spent $220,000 on his private residence at the church — the rectory they call it." Denis caught himself, "I'm sorry, Your Grace. You already know what it's called."

Bishop Barbarito flexed his hands as if he was stretching them, then pointed his index finger at Denis's chest. "Please. Continue," he said.

"There's $50,000 or so that he spent — on what we're not quite sure. However, it might have been on . . ." Denis hesitated. Then he cleared his throat. "It appears Father Guinan might have a girlfriend. Again, we're not sure."

Bishop Barbarito rolled his eyes and sighed heavily.

"And recently Father Guinan spent $325,000 on property in Port St. Lucie. He also spent $5,365 on homeowner fees," said Denis.

"On the Port St. Lucie property?"

"No. On another property that he owns in Juno Beach. Apparently, he bought it some years ago, before he came to St. Vincent's."

The bishop nodded.

"Another $15,000 was spent by Father Guinan on dental and medical bills. And $30,000 or so went directly into his bank account. We haven't been able to trace it yet, so I don't know what it went for," explained Denis.

"Is that all?" asked Bishop Barbarito.

"No, Your Grace," said Denis. "There's another $170,000 missing, but we can't trace it either. Perhaps the police will be able to. It was probably frittered away on his vacations. Apparently, he likes to go to Las Vegas and the Bahamas."

Bishop Barbarito's cheeks glowed red in his pale face, as if he'd just been slapped. "Yes, the police," said the bishop, looking at the wall behind Denis.

Both men were unaware that just thirty days before Colleen Head had taken her two-year-old anonymous letter from her file drawer. She had mailed two copies of it. One to the Palm Beach diocese, where a secretary had filed it in her "nonsense" file. She hadn't known what to do with it. Since it was anonymous, she had decided it was a bad joke — written by some prankster. The other had gone to the Palm Beach Police Department, who had already begun an investigation.

"I'm sorry, Your Grace," said Denis in a quiet voice.

"As we all are," said the bishop, focusing on Denis. "What about Father Skehan?"

"It would seem he is responsible for pilfering the other $8 million," said Denis.

"*Stealing* is the word," said the bishop in a blunt voice. "Pilfering implies taking a candy bar from a convenience store."

Denis nodded. "So far we know that Father Skehan purchased two luxury homes for around $1 million. He spent approximately $4 or $500,000 on rare coins — we have photocopies of the receipts. And $134,000 went to Father

Skehan's girlfriend."

Bishop Barbarito dropped his chin to his chest, exhaling grimly. "Another girlfriend?" he asked as he lifted his head.

"So it seems, Your Grace," said Denis. "We can't account for the rest of the $8 million. But we know — for certain — that it is missing."

The bishop got up from his chair and stood behind his desk. "Thank you, Denis. You have been very thorough. I know what I have to do."

Denis gathered his papers, nodded, and left.

Bishop Gerald Barbarito sat behind his desk for a long time, thinking. Then, reaching for his phone, he called the Palm Beach Police Department. He told them what the diocesan audit had exposed. The Palm Beach Police told him they already had an investigation under way. They would keep him informed.

Next the bishop called Father Francis Guinan, who was available this time. Bishop Barbarito told Father Guinan that he had just been removed as the pastor of St. Vincent Ferrer Church.

Father Guinan wanted to know why.

Bishop Barbarito said, "For embezzlement of church funds."

Father Guinan demanded to know what proof the bishop had. Bishop Barbarito told Father Guinan what the accountant had just told him.

Father Guinan shouted about "private business and invasion of privacy."

Bishop Barbarito listened in silence. When Father Guinan's tirade ended, the bishop said, "Your position as pastor of St. Vincent Ferrer Church is ended. I have removed you."


28

"You can't do that," yelled Father Guinan. "I won't allow you to set me aside. Not without proof. Which you don't have. All you have is some vague allegations."

In his office, Bishop Barbarito stood straight. "As bishop, I may remove any priest without cause or explanation."

Father Guinan stopped shouting because he knew it was true. Finally, he said, "I won't be removed. I'm retiring instead." He slammed the phone down.

Nothing happened for sixteen months while the Palm Beach Police investigated. Father Skehan and Father Guinan knew that they were suspected of grand theft by embezzlement and that they were being investigated. Father Skehan was now seventy-nine. He didn't care much what happened to him anymore. Depressed despite his wealth, he had discovered that money didn't make him happy.

At the age of sixty-two, Father Guinan cared. Yet, at the same time, he arrogantly dismissed the Palm Beach Police as barely educated fools who had no concrete evidence against him and no prospects of getting any. Besides, Guinan believed that any money that had come into *his* church was *his*. A mighty sense of priestly privilege filled him. He actually believed priests were immune to the rules and laws that applied to ordinary people. In his own eyes, he was anything but ordinary — he was exceptional.

In August 2006, Father Skehan booked a flight to Ireland. He was going back to the old country to visit his roots. Dublin called to the Irish in him, like the Sirens had called to Ulysses. He would live in his cottage, drink at his pub, be with his people.

Before he left, Skehan contacted a big-name, highly recommended, criminal defense attorney. If charges were filed, he wanted to be ready. After hearing his story, the attorney told him not to worry. When the time came, if the time came, the attorney would launch a flurry of counterpunches, which would stun the authorities. The attorney also explained to Father Skehan the concept of the statute of limitations. Essentially, it meant that Father Skehan could not be charged with, or be held criminally liable for, any crime that had taken place more than five years ago. Only what had happened in the past five years — since 2001 — was pertinent to any investigation.

When he heard that, Father Skehan relaxed. He felt as if someone had lifted a grand piano off his shoulders.

The attorney then told him that, even if charges were filed, unless the prosecution had an airtight case against him, the attorney could plea bargain. In other words, they could swing a deal with the authorities. At the most, the attorney went on, Skehan might receive a little community service, a fine, and maybe probation for a few years. No big deal, really.

The attorney's name was Ken Johnson. Skehan gave him a fat retainer fee — just in case. Father Skehan got on a plane to Ireland.

Meanwhile, Father Guinan underwent a crisis: the more time that passed with nothing happening, the more worried he became. Courage failed him, as did his sense of priestly privilege. Finally, he'd had enough. He decided to get out of town while the getting was good. It was either that or have a nervous breakdown. He packed his bags and then picked up his girlfriend — who had been his secretary at St. Patrick's Church before he took over St. Vincent's — and they left for a long vacation. First they traveled to Ireland, then Singapore. After Singapore got boring, they booked passage on a luxury cruise ship to Australia.

On September 29, 2006, Father Skehan returned home. His trip to Ireland had refreshed him. It had been good to see the green hills of Ireland, to smell the air of leprechauns, to hear the muscular Irish dialect of his youth. But after about six weeks, he had found himself longing for Florida sunshine and a good steak. So he'd packed his bags.

As his flight landed at Miami International Airport, Father Skehan's spirits soared higher as the plane descended lower. As Skehan walked off the plane into the concourse, the moist warmth of Florida kissed his skin. Even the airport's air conditioners couldn't neutralize the old familiar feeling.

Father Skehan passed quickly through customs and immigration. All he had to do now was collect his bags and find a cab. As he turned to make his way to the escalators, four men converged on him. One of the men flashed a badge and handed him a folded piece of paper. Then the man rattled off a series of sentences he had obviously memorized.

"Do you understand your rights?" asked the policeman.

"Yes," said Father Skehan.

"Okay," said the policeman. "You're charged with grand larceny. Let's go, please."

One of the men cuffed Father Skehan's hands behind his back. Then they walked out of the airport into a waiting police vehicle. As Skehan sat stunned in the back of the vehicle, the police asked him questions.

"Did you steal large sums of money from the St. Vincent Ferrer Catholic Church while you were the pastor of the church?"

"Yes," said Father Skehan.

"How much money did you steal?"

"I don't know," said Skehan, shrugging. His cuffed hands

were cutting into his back. "It was a mountain of money. I don't know how much it was. I never bothered to keep track."

"Why?"

"Why what?" asked Skehan. He wondered if he should be telling them this.

"Why did you steal from your own church?"

"Because I never got paid enough," Skehan told the investigator.

The investigator stared at him.

"I was the CEO of a multi-million-dollar company — St. Vincent's," explained Skehan. "I was never properly compensated for my abilities." He shifted in his seat, trying to ease the discomfort of sitting with handcuffs on. "The money was mine. I deserved it."

"So you admit that you stole the money?"

"Yes. I misappropriated money," blurted Skehan. He stopped. After a moment, he said, "I have nothing more to say. Not without my attorney being present."

The police took Skehan to the Palm Beach jail, where they booked him. They took his fingerprints. Then he was strip-searched, a humiliating ordeal. After he received his jail clothing, a sheriff's deputy escorted him to a holding cell. On the way to the cell, the deputy handed him a brown paper bag. Once the cell door closed with a clang, Father Skehan opened the bag. Two peanut butter and jelly sandwiches and a mushy red apple. This was his lunch.

An hour later another deputy arrived, unlocked his cell door, and escorted him to a phone. Skehan called Ken Johnson, his attorney. Johnson told him to relax. He'd be released in twenty-four hours. The deputy took Skehan back to his cell.

Six hours later a deputy led Skehan to the release area, where his attorney and another man waited. The other man was his bail bondsman. He was Hispanic and dressed in an expensive suit, no tie. Sliding a sheaf of papers in front of Skehan, he instructed the priest to sign his name at the bottom of each page.

As he signed, Skehan looked at his attorney. "What is all this?" he asked.

"Your bail was set at $400,000," said Johnson. "These documents are necessary to obtain your release. If you don't sign, the bondsman won't front the money for your bail."

"Oh," said Skehan, scribbling his name.

Father Skehan waited another thirty minutes before he was allowed to change into his own clothes. Then they let him go.

His attorney drove him home, telling him not to speak to anyone. "No interviews. No phone conversations. No communication with anyone other than me," said Johnson. "If the police come around asking you for statements, refer them to me."

Father Skehan nodded.

Meanwhile, a warrant for the arrest of Father Francis Guinan had already been issued. However, the police could not locate him and assumed he had taken flight. He was on the run as far as the Palm Beach Police were concerned.

Guinan wasn't really on the run. Rather, he was trying to avoid arrest as long as possible. In Australia, he heard through friends in Florida that the police were looking for him and that they had a warrant for his arrest. Scared, Guinan told his girlfriend what he had learned. Being a practical and calculating woman, she was not surprised.

After thinking about it for a moment, she told him, "You have two choices, Frank. Either negotiate a surrender, or take the money and run." Giving him a direct look, she added, "And since they've probably already seized your accounts or soon will, you're pretty much screwed."

Guinan blinked rapidly, trying to understand what he'd just been told. She was right. Still in avoidance mode, he suggested they have lunch. As they ate fresh crab sandwiches washed down with a nutty Chardonnay, Guinan said little. Mostly, he listened to his girlfriend as she counseled him on the ins and outs of what kind of bargain he might be able to swing. As they finished the meal, he knew what to do.

Back in their luxury suite at the hotel, Guinan called David Roth in Miami. A high-profile criminal defense attorney, Roth represented many hoity-toity clients, one of whom was U.S. Representative, Mark Foley.

The priest and the attorney discussed his predicament. Roth was aware of the problem because Guinan's photo was all over the news. The Miami television stations were giving it lots of airplay, accompanied by dramatic details of the magnitude of the crime. Roth told Father Guinan that he could negotiate a very civilized surrender for him. Roth assured the priest he would be arrested, booked, and released on his own recognizance. Bail would be reasonable. What was high was Roth's fee. The bargaining process with the Florida state attorney would begin as soon as Roth's retainer had been wired to Miami.

"You're hired," said Guinan. "I'll wire the funds immediately."

After he hung up the phone, Guinan wired the money.

"Fucking lawyers are greedy as hell," he snarled to his girlfriend. Looking out the window of his luxury suite, he saw people swimming in areas protected by shark nets and patrol boats. "They make great white sharks look like fucking goldfish."

Three days later, on September 30 — one day after the arrest of Father Skehan — Guinan flew to Miami International Airport. He arrived alone. His girlfriend decided to remain in Australia for an unspecified duration. Police greeted Guinan as he walked off the plane. He was not cuffed; neither was he questioned or read his rights, as he now had legal representation. Transported to the Miami-Dade County Jail, he was booked, and a judge set his bail at $50,000. Hours later, after bond was posted, Father Guinan walked out of the jail.

The next day all hell broke loose.

At a news conference, various police officials and defense attorneys answered questions from the media.

"They were skimming cash out of the offering plates and other donations that came into the church," Jeff Messer said. Messer was the Delray Beach police spokesman. "They were spending some on church projects, and they were spending a lot on themselves, for vacations, buying properties, gambling trips to Las Vegas and the Bahamas, and alleged girlfriends. We can prove several hundred thousand has been spent on personal use by each of them," Messer said. Then he added that a church audit had covered more than four decades that Skehan had served the church.

"Millions of dollars that should have gone to helping the homeless folks or the school itself" didn't, said Amos Rojas Jr., a special agent with the Florida Department of Law Enforcement.

One official stated that Guinan had had an "intimate

relationship" with a former bookkeeper at St. Patrick's Church, where he had served before taking over at St. Vincent's Church. The priest had paid the woman's American Express bills — to the tune of $43,000 — and her son's private school tuition. The money used to pay for these items had been from St. Vincent's and had not been recorded on the church books.

A reporter asked about the criminal charges.

An investigator replied that Skehan was charged with grand theft of $100,000 or more between September 2001 and January 2006. Guinan faced the same charge for embezzlement from September 2003 to April 2005.

Another reporter asked about the figure of $8.6 million. Who took it? What was it spent on?

None of the officials could answer the question, except to say they didn't know where most of the $8.6 million went or how it had been stolen. The investigation was continuing.

Skehan's attorney, Ken Johnson, said he thought the figure of $8.6 million was "oversensationalized. My reading of the probable cause affidavit indicates that the amount of money he's actually accused of misappropriating amounts to about $325,000, which is a far cry from $8.6 million."

The following day Bishop Barbarito issued a statement. The two priests had been placed on administrative leave and did not have permission to exercise their priestly ministries until the criminal matter was resolved.

The same afternoon the media carnival — television reporters and newspaper reporters with their attendant cameramen — descended on St. Vincent Ferrer like locusts on a field of corn. On-the-scene television trucks sprouted coiled antennas, while reporters jostled for position.

Joan Koppins was leaving afternoon mass at St. Vincent's.

For twenty years, she had attended mass on a regular basis there. Pushing her way past the suffocating gauntlet of reporters, who kept asking her questions, she headed for her car. She felt as if she had done something wrong, committed some horrible crime. Tears streaming down her cheeks, she got into her car. Reporters pressed right up to her car window. Wiping her wet cheeks with a tissue, she said, "You can't judge because you haven't walked in their shoes." Then she drove off.

Bubs Bergen told reporters that for a long time church members had suspected Guinan's relationship with that woman.

Jack Kneuer said sadly that he was trying to understand what drove priests to do such things. "I think it was like a little leak in a dike that got bigger and bigger," he said. "Once started, there was no way of stopping."

Annette Benoit felt deceived. "All I kept saying when I heard about this was, 'Why would they do it?' There are so many poor people, so many charities that could have used this money."

On the last day of September 2006 — at Saturday mass — Bishop Barbarito arrived at St. Vincent Ferrer Catholic Church. Standing in front of the altar, the bishop apologized to the church members for the pain the priests had caused. Tall and eloquent and sincere, wearing a flowing black cassock with red piping and a red sash, he oozed holiness.

"I am the bishop of the diocese, and when there's any misdeeds on the part of the priests, and the alleged ones we're looking at, then it's up to me as bishop to apologize," he said. "We are human, and we are going to make mistakes," he went on. "Some mistakes are understandable, and some are very hard to understand. These we're looking at today are very hard to understand. I'm truly, truly, truly sorry. As these allegations give rise to grave concern and possible feelings of betrayal and anger, let us remain steadfast in faith and in the sacramental life of the Church knowing that the power of grace is operative at this time."

The investigation continued for the next two years as prosecutors gathered evidence. The charges against the two priests were amended. Father Skehan was accused of embezzling $370,000, from 2001 to 2006. Father Guinan was accused of embezzling $488,000, from 2003 to 2005.

Skehan, now eighty-two, lived in one of his $500,000 luxury penthouses. He added a new attorney, Scott Richardson, to his defense team. Richardson had vast experience in embezzlement cases and was shrewd. Guinan, who was sixty-five, resided in Juno Beach, traveled throughout Florida, and seemed to have plenty of cash at hand.

The five-year statute of limitations began to hinder the prosecutors. They could not charge the priests for all their crimes. Father Skehan could be committed only for those crimes in the last five years of his stay at St. Vincent's. The prosecutors suspected that Father Guinan had done the same thing at his previous church — St. Patrick's. But again they couldn't go back more than five years. The legal system was working for the priests and against the prosecutors.

The two priests' defense attorneys, David Roth and Scott Richardson, kept asking Palm Beach Circuit Judge Sandra McSorley for postponements of the trial. Their reasons were "the huge amount of paperwork involved and the complexity of the case."

Prosecutors also kept asking for postponement since they were not ready to go to trial. They didn't have enough hard evidence. There really was too much paperwork to sift through. And, like most embezzlement cases, the twists and turns of the maze boggled the mind.

In February 2008, both sides asked Judge McSorley for a continuation of the trial. State Attorney Barry Krischer said, "In order for the lawyers to reach an honorable resolution for their client, whether it's the state or the accused, it requires information. There has not been enough time to accumulate all that information. It has stymied the negotiation process."

The operative word in that statement was *negotiation*. It meant that both sides were trying to cut a deal — a plea bargain. Which meant that the prosecutors were unsure of the strength of their case.

Judge McSorley was surprised and upset by the request. So she postponed her decision on the request for postponement. Instead, she asked the attorneys to give her a time line for when the case might go to trial. She strongly suggested the time line show that the trial would begin in June. "Because of the identified unusual delay in this case," said Judge McSorley, "both the court and the public are entitled to an assurance that there is certainty that this criminal prosecution will in fact conclude in the June 2008 time frame requested by both the prosecutor and defense counsel. In the court's view, unique and extraordinary circumstances require unique and extraordinary measures."

Prosecutor Krischer told Judge McSorley that, if the case went to trial while the defense attorneys said they were not ready, convictions could be overturned on appeal.

Judge McSorley criticized both sides for not preparing quickly enough. Then she added that she would not decide on the request until the time line was forthcoming.

Court was dismissed, and no one knew what was going on.

Prosecutor Krischer huddled his team together for a brainstorming session. They needed to come up with a game plan or risk losing. Ideas were tossed out. Krischer listened to them while he pondered the situation. After about an hour, he decided there was only one thing to do. Taking the floor, he told his team what he had decided. They liked it.

That afternoon Krischer filed court papers dropping the criminal charges against Father Skehan and Father Guinan. The charges would be refiled when the prosecutors were ready to go to trial. Which meant when they had enough evidence to make their case.

In the meantime, the door was open for a plea bargain. If prosecutors thought their case was weak, they could cut the priests a deal. Something was better than nothing.

Krischer spoke to the media, who were shocked and dismayed that the charges had been dropped. What about justice? the reporters wanted to know.

"I've taken it upon myself," said Krischer, "to take control of the case. It is just so the lawyers can get ready."

It was more than that, though. It was a slap in the face to Judge McSorley. It also indicated which way the wind was blowing. A deal would probably be made.

Why? Because morally the priests were guilty of grand theft by embezzlement. However, technically the priests had been the spiritual, administrative, and legal leaders of the church. In other words, Father Skehan and Father Guinan had been in charge of the money. Their attorneys could reasonably argue that they had every right to spend church funds as they saw fit. Priests had to live somewhere, and all priests at all churches took vacations.

The prosecution would then argue that $500,000 penthouses and gambling junkets to Las Vegas and the Bahamas went far beyond what most priests received.

The defense attorneys would pounce on that like starving animals on raw meat. That's weak, they would shout, because some churches were rich and some were poor. There was no hard-and-fast standard. Skehan and Guinan had served rich churches. So their perks had been expensive.

If the prosecutors brought up the girlfriends, they would be laughed out of court. A girlfriend, even for a priest, was not a crime. And then the defense would point out that the cash gifts to the women had come from the priests' personal funds — charitable acts, which priests were supposed to do.

Which left a deal as the only option.

The priests would plead guilty to lesser charges and walk away from the whole thing.

*Author's note:* On March 24, 2009, Circuit Judge Jeffrey Colbath sentenced Father Skehan to fourteen months in prison. The sentence was the result of a plea bargain.

Father Skehan's attorney, the Diocese of Palm Beach, and even one of the prosecutors had requested that Father Skehan's punishment consist only of probation. Judge Colbath dismissed the requests, saying, "The crime of the defendant was pure greed unmasked. There is not a shred of moral necessity to excuse the defendant's crime."

The next day, March 25, 2009, Circuit Judge Krista Marx sentenced Father Francis Guinan to four years in prison. The jury had found Father Guinan guilty of second-degree felony grand theft, which, in technical terms, meant Father Guinan was guilty of stealing between $20,000 and $100,000.

He had, in fact, stolen much, much more than $100,000. But such is the power of the church.

Throughout the trial, Guinan's attorney tried to shift the blame from the priest to the church. The attorney inisisted that the church's lax accounting practices were responsible for the missing money. No theft had taken place.

Before sentencing occurred, Father Guinan made a brief statement to the court. He apologized to anyone that he had disappointed. Then he asked, "Isn't the month that I've been incarcerated more than enough punishment?"

After it was all over, Guinan's attorney, Richard Barlow, commented on the difference between the sentences given to the two priests. "It's indicative of secret deals that were struck behind the scenes. And it demonstrates the bitterness and anger that the prosecutors have against Father Guinan for exercising his right to go to trial."

# CHAPTER 2

## SINS OF THE FATHERS

GREENWICH, CONNECTICUT, SPRING 1998. A great idea had just popped into the head of long-time swindler Martin Frankel. He needed to become more religious.

If he could link up with the Roman Catholic Church, all his problems would be over. He could set up some kind of charitable foundation as a front, with an account at the Vatican bank. Then he could move funds around at will and buy up more insurance companies. Big ones. After he liquidated their assets, he'd move their money into the Vatican account. From there, he could move it into his own accounts as needed. The best part was this: no one would dare question him because no one would question the Church. It was perfect.

Besides, it fit the image Frankel had of himself.

Reaching out a pale, thin arm, he punched an intercom button. He was sitting in the home office of his luxurious mansion. Leaning forward, he said, "Mona, could you come in here?" He didn't wait for an answer. His "girls" always did what he asked. Supposedly, the "girls" were secretaries or administrative assistants. But everyone knew what they really were: women whom Frankel was attracted to and wanted to sleep with. So he hired them and paid them tons of money to be nothing more than gofers.

A plump woman about thirty years old walked through the doors into the so-called trading room, which was illuminated only by the eerie glow of forty computer monitors. Arranged in a large circle, the monitors perched on card tables, desks, and work tables.

"What's up, Marty?" asked Mona.

Frankel swiveled his chair around, looking up at her. "I've got an assignment for you," he said. "I want you to get me some books on Catholicism. Lots of books. I want to study up on the subject." He turned back to three monitors in front of him.

Mona waited patiently. She knew how his mind worked, flitting from thing to thing like a bee buzzing from flower to flower.

Flicking his fingers over a keyboard, Frankel watched as a new set of data appeared before his eyes. Nodding to himself, he glanced over at Mona. "Lots of books," he said. "And I want all you can find on St. Francis of Assisi — you know, the monk back in the 1200s who gave everything he owned to the poor and started his own religious order." He reached for a bottle of purified water and uncapped it. Taking a sip, he said, "Did you know the Franciscans governed their lives by two principles? Simplicity and poverty."

Mona didn't know that, but she didn't care either. As far as she was concerned, poverty was for the birds. And life boiled down to two choices: you could be rich, or you could be poor. She preferred rich. Which was why she liked Marty.

Mona nodded. "Okay, Marty. I'll get right on it." She left, closing the double doors carefully.

Frankel picked up one of the phones in front of him and dialed a number from memory. "Tom," he said, hearing a deep voice on the other end. "It's David."

Tom was Tom Corbally, a seventy-seven-year-old pimp. Only Corbally didn't deal in sex — he dealt in contacts. Specifically, business contacts to people in high places.

Charisma poured out of Corbally. It was his talent and his weakness. He would enter a room dressed in suits from the best tailors in the world — Savile Row — smoking a hand-rolled Cuban cigar, and immediately attract the most beautiful women. He was magnetic. His voice was a sexy rumble, so deep "it made Johnny Cash sound like a soprano." He knew everyone, but no one knew what he did or where his money came from. When asked, he told people he was "a business consultant."

Hanging out with Lee Iacocca, Henry Kissinger, Larry Tisch, Barbara Walters, Rita Hayworth, and Heidi Fleiss cemented his reputation as a player. He knew other people too. Some of them were very suspicious, such as Stephen Ward, a medical doctor, pimp, and spy. Through Ward, Corbally came to know Christine Keeler, an international call girl — a groupie to rich and powerful men. She bedded John Profumo and Yevgeny Ivanov. Profumo was the secretary for war in Great Britain, and Ivanov was the Soviet naval attaché. For some reason, in 1963 Corbally blabbed this information to the U.S. ambassador to Great Britain. The ambassador used this scandalous news to force the resignation of England's prime minister.

All these circumstances caused the FBI in the 1960s to start taking note of Corbally. They began a file on him. In keeping with Corbally's reputation, the FBI called the file "Bowtie." Nothing ever came of it, but some people wonder what was in it.

"David," said Corbally, "it's always good to talk with you."

Frankel had many aliases. He found them necessary in his line of work. Martin Frankel was also known as Michael Fiore, Mick Gates, Martin King, Mike King, Eric Jensen, Mark Shuki, David Stevens, Eric Stevens, Will Stevens, and Steve Rothschild. There was no pattern to their use. He picked them whimsically. Because of that, he couldn't keep them straight. Which explained why he answered the phone with "What can I do for you?"

Right now, though, Frankel was "David Rosse." He made a mental note to himself to remember that. To pull this off, he needed to remain Rosse for a while.

Corbally knew him as David Rosse, eccentric billionaire.

"Yeah. Listen, Tom," said Frankel, "I've decided to start my own charity. In fact, I want it to be the biggest and best charity around. To do that, I feel like it should be affiliated with the Catholic Church, which is the biggest and best around too. That would give it the cachet I envision for it."

Without missing a beat, Corbally jumped right in. "You know, I used to be an altar boy years ago. What's more, I know a lot of people who know a lot of people in the Vatican." He paused as if deep in thought. "Let me make a few calls," said Corbally in a confident tone. "I'll see what I can do for you. It shouldn't take me long at all."

Corbally made a call to Fausto Fausti, who lived in Rome and knew how to get things done. Corbally explained the situation to Fausti, telling him that a very eccentric billionaire wanted to give away a lot of money but insisted that it be done through a Catholic charity. Fausti liked the idea, primarily because it meant he could charge hefty fees for his services as a consultant. He told Corbally he'd check around.

Next Corbally called Thomas Bolan, who lived in New York. Bolan, a well-known, high-profile attorney, was considered a smooth operator. He was also a staunch Catholic.

The two men met for lunch at Harry Cipriani's, a lavish Venetian restaurant at the Sherry Netherland in New York City. Cipriani's reeked of money and power and deals made over single-malt whiskey. In tailored suits costing more than most people made in a month, the two players ate at Corbally's usual table.

"My friend's name," said Corbally, taking a sip of whiskey, "is David Rosse. He's quite a unique character." He looked around the restaurant, nodding to powerful men he knew. Wealth and power satisfied him. Smiling at Bolan, he said, "Not only is he rich as Midas, but he's most selfless." Corbally winked at Bolan. "Along with being more than a little eccentric."

Bolan smiled and nodded. He knew the type.

"Anyway," said Corbally, "he wants to spend the rest of his life helping the poor and the needy." He took another gulp of his drink and leaned back in his chair. "To do that correctly, he wants to work with and through the Church."

Bolan nodded in approval. "That's the best way."

"That's what I told him," said Corbally. He wiped the moisture from the side of his glass with a napkin. "I also told him that you were well connected in the Church. And that perhaps you could suggest the proper way to approach the Vatican."

Bolan sat listening intently. He liked what he was hearing. He could also see many advantages — for everyone. To Bolan, the word *advantage* was synonymous with money.

"Would you be interested in helping Rosse fulfill his dream?" said Corbally. Then he tossed off the rest of his drink.

"It just so happens," Bolan said, smiling, "that I have a friend who knows all the right people in the Vatican."

Satisfaction pumped through Corbally. He signaled the waiter for another round of drinks.

"Father Peter Jacobs," said Bolan. "That's my friend's name. But most people just call him Father Jake. He knows everybody who's worth knowing."

Corbally smiled and nodded. There was a pause as their waiter placed two tumblers of scotch on the rocks on the table.

"I mean everybody," said Bolan. "One of his frequent visitors was Princess Grace."

Corbally's eyes widened.

"Yeah, I know," agreed Bolan. "Father Jake would take her to dinner in the Bowery, if you can believe it. Other times they'd go to Le Cirque or to '21.' She invited him over to Monaco, put him up in the palace. He said mass for her in the palace chapel."

"Precisely the man we need," said Corbally in a voice fat with delight.

Bolan wore a huge grin.

Corbally raised his glass to Bolan's. "To Father Jake," said Corbally.

"And to David Rosse's money," said Bolan.

They beamed smiles at each other.

Corbally decided the time was right for Bolan to meet David Rosse. They were driven to Greenwich by Corbally's chauffeur in a black Mercedes. The car and the chauffeur were paid for by Marty Frankel, aka David Rosse.

Marty owned two homes in Greenwich. In reality, they were mansions. The houses sat next to each other on four-acre plots. Each cost about $3 million. Both houses had elite chefs, maids, housekeepers, and grounds crew. Marty lived in and ran his "business" out of one house, while his entourage lived in the other.

As the Mercedes whispered through the front gates and onto a long circular drive, Bolan noticed $2 million worth of luxury cars parked here, there, and everywhere. The sight of money.

In the foyer of the house, Bolan and Corbally stood in the middle of thousands of books. All on Catholicism. Bolan was impressed. If Rosse had actually read them all, he'd be even more impressed.

Corbally said, "Excuse me for a minute, will ya', Tom? I'm going to go in and have a few words with David. Then I'll bring you in. Okay?"

"Sure," said Bolan. "Take your time." He walked over to the bookshelves for a closer look.

No one knows what Corbally and Rosse talked about, but more than likely Corbally wanted to prep the meeting with do's and don'ts. He realized he was dealing with a major flake and wanted to caution Rosse not to make any outlandish statements.

When Bolan entered the so-called trading room, it took his eyes a moment to adjust to the lack of light. When they did, he saw a slender figure silhouetted in front of dozens of computer monitors. The guy looked like a street person, unshaven, wearing oversized jeans. Thick glasses perched on his nose, exaggerating his eyes like those of a cartoon character peering through a fishbowl.

Corbally and Bolan sat in a couple of the dozen leather recliners scattered around the room. No formal introductions and no small talk.

As soon as the two suits sat down, David started talking. "I've made a lot of money — mostly through trading stocks. My record is 90% right picks. With all my money, now I want to help those less fortunate — the most unfortunate creatures in the world . . . the poor are. Even though I'm a Jew, my hero, my spiritual guide, you might say, has always been Saint Francis of Assisi. Once I saw that movie by Zeffirelli — *Brother Sun, Sister Moon* — I just knew. I sat through it six times. The only people in the theater were me and some nuns."

As the guy went on and on, Bolan realized he was more than eccentric. He was a nut case. But obviously a genius whose heart was in the right place. Real compassion oozed out of the guy.

"I can make big money for the Church," David continued. "In the billions of dollars range. What I want to do is this: I give $55 million to one of the Church's charities, with the understanding that I maintain control of $50 million — for trading purposes, you understand. Five million goes to the charity. They keep that." David stopped talking and looked at Bolan.

Bolan cleared his throat, then said, "I can see and can appreciate what you're trying to do. It's very commendable. In fact, it's downright nice." Bolan smiled and clasped his hands in front of him. "Might I suggest this? Why not simply donate the money to some Catholic organization? Like, say,

St. John's University. That would certainly meet all your requirements." St. John's University was Bolan's alma mater.

David shook his head. "No, no, that won't do it. To make more money for the Church, I have to have control of the money. That way I can buy more and make more. And the Church will make more, you understand." He looked down at the floor, then up at Bolan. "I want to deal directly with the pope and through the Vatican. Because, if you can't trust the pope and the Catholic Church, whom can you trust?"

"I see your point," Bolan said, nodding. "And I'd like to be involved. Let me think about the proper ways and means. And I'll let you know what I come up with."

Sitting in the back of the splendid Mercedes as it headed back to New York, Bolan turned to Corbally. "Rosse seems like a likable guy, very sincere, very shy. He's so shy I feel sorry for him."

Corbally chuckled. "Yeah. He's a bit off center. But don't feel too sorry for him. The guy's worth billions." Corbally flicked a piece of lint off his pants. "Money can buy a lot of happiness."

Bolan laughed and agreed.

Meanwhile, Fausto Fausti was stirring things up in Rome. He talked with Father Christopher Zielinski, the prior (person in charge) at a monastic church in San Miniato al Monte, Italy. Zielinski was also a director of a charity called the Genesis Center. It had just what they were looking for: Vatican sponsorship and an account at the Vatican bank.

Father Zielinski put Fausti in touch with Michele Spike, another director of the Genesis Center. She was also an attorney. Even though Fausti did his best to impress Spike, dropping the names of Lee Iacocca and Bill Fugazy, the deal didn't pan out. According to Fausti, Iacocca and Fugazy were both on Rosse's board of directors. This, of course, was a lie. There was no board of directors. Spike smelled something fishy. Fausti represented some unknown person who wanted to give away millions of dollars. But at the same time, Mr. Unknown wanted to control the money. In other words, Spike thought, he wanted to *use* the charity. It stunk of deception.

She told Fausti the Genesis Center could not and would not participate.

Back in New York, Bolan made a call to Father Peter Jacobs, a seventy-two-year-old extravagant priest. Father Jacobs was also known as Father Jake, the Jewish Priest, and Reverend to the Stars, because he attended all the high-society events and knew all the celebrities in town. Father Jacobs liked to do his own thing.

Around 1980, he opened a fancy restaurant in New York's theater district. Called The Palatine, the restaurant attracted celebrity patrons of the time, such as Bianca Jagger and Yoko Ono. When the archdiocese ordered him to close his restaurant, Father Jacobs ignored the order. This, of course, ticked off the wrong people, and in 1982 the archdiocese suspended him, denying him the authority to say mass, perform weddings, and anoint the sick. A few years later he finally closed The Palatine. The archdiocese gave him back part of his priestly functions. Father Jacobs, though, paid no attention. He still did as he pleased. He hung out and partied with Jackie Kennedy, Walter Cronkite, Grace Kelly, and Norman Mailer.

Luckily, Father Jake knew the right people in the Church too. He enjoyed favorite son status at the Vatican, having been a close personal friend of Pope Paul VI.

When Bolan called him, Father Jake was semi-retired, living in Rome, where he was a familiar sight driving around on a blue Vespa while wearing his cassock. As his tassles streamed out behind him, and the black skirt of his cassock whipped back, he waved and honked at everyone.

During their conversation, Bolan explained what David Rosse — the eccentric, generous billionaire — wanted to do. Once Father Jake heard the proposal, he was in. He told Bolan that he had helped Milton Petrie do the same kind of thing years ago. The publicity-shy owner of an apparel empire, which included Stuart's, G&G, Jean Nicole, and Toys 'R' Us, Petrie had wanted to donate many of his millions to charity too. Father Jake had advised him. Petrie had shown his gratitude by buying Father Jake a Volkswagen. Petrie thought gratitude should be more than a feeling — it should be real, something touchable. Father Jake agreed wholeheartedly.

"I know just the person," said Father Jake.

"Who's that?" asked Bolan.

"A close friend of mine, Monsignor Emilio Colagiovanni. He's a Vatican insider. Used to be on the Roman Rota," explained Father Jake.

"The what?" said Bolan.

"The Roman Rota. It's a religious appeals court."

"Oh," said Bolan. "So he was a judge?"

"Yes."

"That's even better," Bolan said, impressed. This was great. Not only was the guy a Vatican insider, but he also used to be a judge. You couldn't get much more respectable than that.

Colagiovanni was a fat-faced, rolly-polly man who wore

his thinning hair in a bad comb-over. And he had sat on the Vatican court of appeals, called the Roman Rota. At the present moment, he was editor-in-chief and publisher of a canonical law review. Published by the Monitor Ecclesiasticus Foundation, which Colagiovanni ran, the review was small potatoes. In reality, so was the foundation, which boasted a few hundred dollars and a staff of one — Colagiovanni. *Monitor Ecclesiasticus* was not an official organ of the Vatican; however, once upon a time, one of the previous popes had bestowed his blessing on it. But what *Monitor Ecclesiasticus* did have was a Vatican bank account.

Conveniently, at that very moment, Monsignor Colagiovanni was in Cleveland, Ohio, where he was visiting family. When Father Jake called him, Colagiovanni, intrigued by what he heard, agreed to fly to New York a few days later. The money for his first-class airfare came from one of Martin Frankel's various bank accounts. Most of these accounts were not in Frankel's name. Instead, they were controlled by front companies, which in turn were controlled by Frankel. In this manner, he maintained his anonymity.

Father Jake flew first-class from Rome. Bolan picked him up in a chauffeur-driven Mercedes paid for by Frankel. Another chauffeur-driven Mercedes picked up Colagiovanni. All three men converged on Greenwich for a meeting with the genius — the money man — Martin Frankel. All three men — Bolan, Father Jake, and Monsignor Colagiovanni — knew him as David Rosse.

Seated in his trading room, in front of almost one hundred computer monitors, Rosse unleashed his same old spiel: how much he admired the Catholic Church, how he venerated Saint Francis of Assisi, and how he wanted to give the Church $55 million.

Colagiovanni almost swooned with delight. Dollar signs danced before his eyes. He couldn't let this opportunity get away. If he brought that kind of money into the Church's coffers, he'd be hobnobbing with the princes of the Church in no time. Raising his index finger in front of his face, he said, "What a wonderful gesture you have decided to make." He glanced at the other three conspirators. "I would be honored to aid you in this blessed venture."

Rosse smiled as he washed his hands with waterless antibacterial soap. He kept a bottle of the stuff with him at all times. Germs were everywhere. As soon as he shook hands with anyone, he used it.

Father Jake, who looked like a Jewish heavyweight boxer whose nose had been broken too many times, leaned forward. He was pleased that Colagiovanni was pleased.

"An idea of such beauty should be presented to those who will appreciate it," said Colagiovanni, looking at David. Colagiovanni made extravagant gestures with his hands as he continued, "Two men: Monsignor Gianfranco Piovano. He is very high up in the Secretariat of State. And Bishop Francesco Salerno. Who is *the* economic expert in the Vatican. Both of them dear friends of mine. With men such as these, the dream will become reality." As he finished, the monsignor raised his hands on high, gazing up at heaven. His face sparkled with heavenly blessing.

Father Jake brought things down to Earth. "Now," he said. "Let's talk about the $5 million and what should be done with it. Boys Town of Italy has been a burden on my heart for some time. I would like to see the lion's share go to them. They do great work for the orphans."

"They do, they do," agreed Colagiovanni. He lifted an index finger, urging wisdom and prudence. "Yet with all humility I must add that my own foundation, *Monitor Ecclesiasticus*, is also worthwhile — and is playing an integral part in all of this."

Father Jake scowled, making a dismissive motion with his hand. "Yes, I guess it is. But think of the children. They are the future." He gazed at Rosse to see if he was thinking of the children.

"Well," said Bolan. "I have a favorite too. Perhaps we should just divide it in three equal portions. That would be the fair way."

Colagiovanni looked at Father Jake, who looked back. Both looked skeptical.

In the end, after a lot of civilized bickering and dickering, the three old guys decided to divide the money as follows: Monitor Ecclesiasticus Foundation (MEF) would receive $3.5 million, Boys Town of Italy would get $1.1 million, and the leftover $400,000 would go to Bolan's choice. MEF got the most because, as everyone grudgingly agreed, without its Vatican connections and its Vatican bank account nothing would happen. Since Bolan didn't really care all that much, his charity got the smallest amount. And Father Jake's Italian boys would get a tidy sum. Everyone was happy.

Rosse was going to donate $55 million to MEF. But only $5 million of that would actually change hands. The books would show that $55 million entered the MEF bank account — but not really because Rosse would hang on to and control the remaining $50 million. And that would happen only if they could get the Vatican to buy into the program, which they hadn't done yet.

Not one of the three old men seemed to realize that what they were talking about was fraud. Blinded by greed, they looked the other way.

David Rosse, aka Martin Frankel, realized it. That was for sure. He was desperately counting on it. Since 1992, he'd been running a classic Ponzi scheme, taking money from five insurance companies he controlled and putting it into his own accounts. Then he cooked the books, showing that he had been investing the money. The cooked books reported fantastic profits. And when one of the insurance companies needed money, he simply transferred money from his own accounts back to it. Later he would move it back into his own accounts. It was like an intricate game of musical chairs, only played with money. There wasn't enough money to go around, so he kept moving funds from location to location, hoping he wouldn't be exposed.

Two hundred million dollars — that's how much money Rosse had run through in the past five years. It was almost all gone. He'd blown it on cars, houses, trips, vacations for his girlfriends and staff, and luxurious apartments. And on gifts, which were really hush payments. Corbally, for example, had been given a $5.8 million apartment in New York City — as a retainer fee. Corbally had also received around-the-clock access to a chauffeur-driven Mercedes and first-class airfare.

Rosse required money — right now. Not only had he embezzled $200 million from his own companies, which needed to be replaced, but he also needed money to maintain his flagrant lifestyle. And, to do those two things, he needed lots of fresh money so that his ever-growing Ponzi scheme could continue to feed itself.

The three old guys piled back into their chauffeur-driven cars and left Greenwich. They were eager to get the project under way. The nearness of money motivated them.

Monsignor Colagiovanni flew back to Cleveland, where he immediately put in a call to the Vatican. On August 22, 1998, Bolan boarded a flight to Rome. One of Rosse's "girls" had booked him a splendid suite at the Hotel Hassler.

As the flight took off, Bolan leaned back in his roomy first-class seat and leafed through a fax he had received a few hours earlier from Rosse. The fax outlined the bargain Rosse anticipated making with the Vatican, including "a secret set of bylaws, spelling out exactly my control of the $50 million, that I am the original Grantor of the funds, and spelling out the Vatican's control of the extra $5 million." Furthermore, Rosse explained in the fax, the $50 million under his control would be used as he saw fit. Which meant purchasing more insurance companies to feed his ongoing Ponzi scheme. He didn't want the Vatican thinking they could tell him what to do. In the final paragraph of the fax, Rosse got right to the point: "In each case of every purchase, the Vatican must be prepared to state, if necessary, that the Vatican is the source of funds." In other words, Rosse wanted the Vatican to lie and participate in fraud. When Bolan finished reading the fax, he didn't even blink twice. It seemed perfectly reasonable to him.

Father Jake met Bolan at the airport in Rome. Bolan slept like a baby in his luxury hotel suite. In the morning, he and Father Jake had breakfast. Then Father Jake took him on a private tour of Vatican City. During the tour, it became obvious that Father Jake indeed knew everyone who was anyone.

Later it was time for Bolan's meeting with Bishop Francesco Salerno, the Vatican's go-to guy in financial arrangements. Salerno, whose title was Secretary of the Prefecture of the Holy See's Economic Affairs, was a banking wizard. He was also honest. Highly educated and polished, Salerno spoke excellent English. After listening to Bolan's proposal, Salerno said, "An excellent idea, this charity of yours. Please draft a set of bylaws for your proposed entity; then we'll talk further."

"Right away," said Bolan, smiling. "I'll get my people going on the bylaws immediately."

Bolan and Father Jake hurried back to the hotel, where Bolan placed a call to New York and instructed his people to fax him a template of bylaws. He would change them where necessary, readying them for the bishop.

Father Jake delivered the proposed bylaws to Bishop Salerno's office. A copy was made and sent over to the Vatican's secretary of state, who also had to approve any such arrangement. After examining them, the secretary of state announced to Father Jake that there was a difficulty.

Father Jake contacted Bolan, who raced over for a meeting with Monsignor Gianfranco Piovano. Piovano, young, darkly handsome, and poised, didn't speak much English. So a translator was brought in. Through the translator, Piovano told Bolan two things. First, the Vatican did not deal in insurance companies. Therefore, second, the bargain would not take place until a more permissible method was presented.

Discouraged as they left Piovano's office, Bolan turned to Father Jake and said, "I never thought it would be so difficult to give away $50 million."

What Bolan forgot was that he wasn't giving away $50 million. In reality, he and Father Jake were playing the Vatican for suckers, trying to make it an accomplice in fraud and embezzlement.

Back at his hotel, Bolan phoned David Rosse in Greenwich. "They're not buying it," said Bolan.

"Why not?" asked Rosse, frustrated anger leaking into his voice.

"They don't involve themselves — the Vatican doesn't — in insurance. It's just not done," explained Bolan. "On a happier note, they like the idea. Just not the means. And that means we need to find a way around their objections."

"I understand," said Rosse. "But these delays are irritating, to say the least. You understand?"

Bolan waited while Rosse thought about what to do.

"Fly back as soon as you can," said Rosse. "We'll put our heads together with Corbally. Maybe he can bring some kind of pressure to bear. We need to find a way to make this happen fast."

"Okay," said Bolan. "See you soon." He started packing his bag.

When Corbally, Father Jake, Bolan, and Rosse gathered in Greenwich, Corbally wanted to put political pressure on the Vatican. Corbally knew Robert Strauss, the former U.S. ambassador to Russia. Strauss knew Zbigniew Brzezinski, who used to be President Carter's national security adviser. Brzezinski had a direct line to the pope because both of them were Polish.

Whether Corbally could actually pull this off or not was never tested. Maybe he was just name-dropping again, one of his favorite diversions. But Rosse was all for it, because he believed that the bigger and more respectable the players the less chance there was his ruse would be discovered. Rosse believed in the power of image.

Corbally's plan was never implemented. Monsignor Colagiovanni had a different idea. Why not give the money directly to *Monitor Ecclesiasticus*, which could then direct the money wherever Rosse said?

Impressed with the idea, Rosse sent Bolan and Father

Jake back to Rome. They were to finalize the operation with Colagiovanni, then get it up and running as fast as possible.

Once back in Rome, Father Jake and Bolan met with Monsignor Colagiovanni. For a man who claimed he had no head for business, Father Jake asked pointed questions. "What account will the money go into at the Vatican bank?" he asked the plump monsignor.

Patting his comb-over into place, Colagiovanni said, "The MEF account, of course. I checked, and the account is authorized to receive wire transfers. So there shouldn't be any problems."

Father Jake looked doubtful. "I don't know," he said slowly. "What would happen if the Vatican changed its mind or started to wonder about what's going on? Once the $55 million is in your account, what's to prevent the Vatican from taking control of it?"

Colagiovanni nodded. "I guess it's always a possibility. But I sincerely doubt it would ever happen. I mean why?"

Father Jake didn't say anything. He just picked up the phone and called David Rosse.

Once Rosse heard Father Jake's concerns, he began worrying too. "I'm with you," Rosse told Father Jake. "It's too risky. There has to be a way to secure the funds. Let me think for a second." A few seconds later Rosse said, "Let's do this instead. I'll put $50 million in a Swiss bank and $5 million in the MEF account. Then I'll open another account for a new foundation. We'll call it the Saint Francis of Assisi Foundation. Once that's in place, I'll transfer the $50 million into the MEF account at the Vatican. Then I'll immediately transfer it out of the MEF account and into the Saint Francis account."

What Rosse didn't say was that this fancy juggling act would not only assure his control of the money but also launder it.

"Yeah, that sounds better," agreed Father Jake after hearing it one more time.

Putting his hand over the phone, he explained the idea to Monsignor Colagiovanni.

"Brilliant," said Colagiovanni, nodding vigorously. He quickly patted his hair with his hand. Then he held up his index finger and gave Father Jake a level look. "But," he said, "MEF gets to keep the $5 million. All of it."

"What?" said Father Jake.

Colagiovanni cocked his head and shrugged — take it or leave it. "Without my foundation — without the MEF account, it won't work. I get the $5 million for my trouble. For my risk."

Scowling, Father Jake brought the phone up to his head. "The monsignor wants to keep the $5 million for his trouble," he told Rosse. Father Jake didn't need to say that he didn't like the idea. His tone of voice said it for him.

"Fine, fine, whatever," said Rosse, tired of wasting time. "But remember, the big payoff isn't going to happen overnight. I'm talking potentially billions of dollars here. It could be five or six years before it happens. Be sure to make that very clear to the others."

"Okay," said Father Jake. After hanging up, he relayed the message about being patient to the others. He especially enjoyed telling Colagiovanni to park his obvious greed in the garage of patience.

Bolan and Father Jake flew back to New York on the Concorde, sitting in first-class seats paid for by Rosse. They sipped champagne. Father Jake, still upset with Colagiovanni's disgraceful greed, drove up to Greenwich to meet with Rosse. When he arrived, he advised Rosse to forget about the MEF idea. They could find some other religious charity or foundation to route the money through. Rosse seriously considered it but in the end didn't pursue it. Time was running out. He needed cash now. Which meant he needed to buy some more insurance companies and liquidate all their assets. Then he could feed part of that money to his own bank accounts, using the rest of the money to buy even more insurance companies. More and bigger ones. If it went as he planned, he would be pulling in billions. And very soon.

As they sat around Rosse's trading room in the Greenwich mansion, Father Jake and Rosse had long heart-to-heart talks on a variety of subjects. Father Jake considered himself to be "David's shrink." He thought there was something in Rosse's past that had left scars on the man. Some emotional trauma perhaps. Whatever it was, the man seemed tormented.

In truth, Marty Frankel, aka David Rosse, did have problems. He suffered from obsessive-compulsive disorder, which explained his constant handwashing and fear of germs. And, as a pathological liar, he couldn't tell the difference between fiction and reality. Mostly, though, guilt was smothering him. He knew what he was doing was wrong and against the law.

Even though he felt for the guy, Father Jake didn't delude himself. He hadn't fallen for the eccentric billionaire spiel. He suspected Rosse was dancing around the ballroom of illegal activity — high-class, sophisticated, white-collar crime. Father Jake wanted to ensure Rosse's success: if Rosse made money, then he would make money. Father Jake had an idea to do that.

"There are many, many deserving people in the world," he told David. "They're everywhere. In every country, every city. It's like Jesus said, 'The poor you shall have with you always.'"

"I suppose there are," said Rosse.

"Those who have should help those who have not, anyway as much as they can," Father Jake said. He held up a large hand to stop the expected protest. "And I know, I know, that one person can't do it all. But if all 'the haves' helped just one of the 'have nots' . . . well, most of the suffering would simply fade away."

Rosse walked over to the sink and washed his hands, using a paper towel to turn the faucet on and off. As he dried his hands on another towel, he gave Father Jake an earnest look. "Is there anything I could do right now?" he asked.

"Well," said Father Jake, smiling, "I have a friend — a cardinal actually — who is raising funds for a hospital in Albania. Our Lady of Good Counsel Hospital, it's called. His name is Pio Laghi. He's high up in the Vatican, used to be the pope's personal ambassador to the U.S. It's a very worthwhile cause — all the children in Albania have nowhere —"

"Would a hundred thousand be okay?" Rosse interrupted.

Father Jake said, "That would be wonderful."

"Okay, I'll do it," said Rosse.

Two days later a bank in Switzerland — Banque SCS — transferred $100,000 into Father Jacob's bank account. From there the money was wired to an account in Tirana, Albania.

Not long after these transactions took place, a letter arrived. It was to Father Jake from Cardinal Laghi, who expressed his gratitude for the donation to the hospital. Father Jake smiled as he read it. As he had anticipated, the cardinal, a very powerful man in the Church, captivated by the gift and the wealth it represented, stepped in. Aware of the ongoing negotiations over Rosse's foundation, and being an old hand at Church politics, he knew what to do. He told his fellow cardinals in the Vatican about the donation. Then he asked that Rosse be granted preferential treatment.

Mission accomplished, thought Father Jake. The path had been smoothed a little more.

Father Jake didn't stop there. Let the money flow! He talked Rosse into donating $50,000 to a Catholic charity in Manila. The priests were so grateful that one of them flew from the Philippines to New York City, then drove up to Greenwich. He and Father Jake prayed with Rosse, adding personal prayers for his soul.

After the priest left with Father Jake, Rosse called John Hackney. Supposedly, Hackney was the president of Franklin American Holding Company, which controlled Rosse's five insurance companies. In reality, Hackney was a front. He was Rosse's puppet. Rosse pulled the strings, and Hackney did as he was told. The phone call wasn't about business. Rosse just wanted to talk to someone. "John," said Rosse, cackling like an old woman, "you should have seen it. Two very serious, very ardent priests — praying for my soul. Can you believe that?"

Hackney chuckled because he had to, but he felt uncomfortable. He was a Southern Baptist and didn't have much good to say about Catholics. But still, they were priests. "Well, no, I really can't see that," he said. He knew Martin Frankel as Martin Frankel. He'd never heard of anyone named David Rosse.

"You should have been here," laughed Rosse. "You can buy souls for $50,000 on today's market."

Rosse, for all his psychological issues, wasn't stupid. He needed Father Jake, and he knew it. So he made sure they were best friends.

One day Father Jake was telling a story about his escapades in Rome. How he zipped around here and there on his blue Vespa.

"You could get killed on that thing, in that kind of traffic," said Rosse. "Why don't you let me buy you a car?"

"No," scoffed Father Jake. "I love my scooter."

"I insist," said Rosse. "What kind of car do you want?"

"Well," said Father Jake, thinking about it. "I used to drive Volkswagens. I've had two of them. Both were given to me. One by Milton Petrie, the other by John Revson. You know, the heir to Revlon, the cosmetics company." He looked at Rosse to determine if he was dazzled by the names. Father Jake certainly was.

"Okay," said Rosse. "A Volkswagen it is. I'll have them get a Mercedes engine and put it in the Volkswagen to make it stronger."

"That's crazy," said Father Jake. "A plain old Volkswagen would be just fine."

Rosse shrugged. "What color?"

"Blue, like my scooter," suggested Father Jake.

"Okay. One blue Volkswagen," Rosse said.

At the same time, Father Jake started receiving $3,300 per month from Rosse — for services rendered.

Rosse also kept the rest of his "team" happy. Colagiovanni would receive the $5 million when the scheme began, but Rosse also wrote him long letters in which Rosse flattered Colagiovanni for his piety. In reality, it was nothing more than flattery. Rosse was using the monsignor, and the monsignor was using Rosse.

In one of his letters, Rosse told Colagiovanni the story of his life and bragged about the 19.3% profits his insurance companies' bond trades had produced that year. More lies. None of the life-story he related was true; he borrowed it all from people he knew. And his insurance companies did no trading of any type and had never shown a profit — except for those on cooked books.

At Rosse's request, Tom Corbally called Bolan. "David wants you to send a bill. He thinks you've done a great job."

"Thanks," said Bolan. When he got off the phone, he made up an invoice for $50,000. Then he faxed it to Rosse in Greenwich.

When he saw the invoice, Rosse smiled and shrugged. He transferred $100,000 to Bolan's account, twice the amount Bolan had asked for. A few weeks later he transferred another $75,000 to Bolan's account.

By October 1998, the scheme was ready to go. The Saint Francis of Assisi Foundation had been chartered in the British Virgin Islands. The foundation listed as advisory board members the old standbys Walter Cronkite and Lee Iacocca. This was not true. What was true, however, was that $55 million would be contributed to the Monitor Ecclesiasticus Foundation, which would then turn around and donate $50 million to the Saint Francis of Assisi Foundation. The foundation would use the money to "serve and help the poor and alleviate suffering."

In actuality, the just-laundered money would be used to buy more insurance companies, which would then be looted by Rosse to buy more insurance companies . . . on and on and on. In the end — ideally — Rosse would have billions of dollars of embezzled money, all the result of an elaborate Ponzi scheme.

Rosse now needed insurance companies to buy. He

enlisted Tom Corbally to help him. Corbally, though, didn't know anything about insurance companies. His specialty was schmoozing. So he contacted a guy named Larry Martin, an investment banker in commercial real estate. Once upon a time, Martin had been an attorney but had found real estate much more lucrative. There was more money to be made, and it was a lot easier.

Rosse put Martin on a retainer of $100,000 a month. To run his end of the deal, Martin took on Thomas F. Quinn, a slick operator from way back. Quinn had been convicted of fraud and had done time in federal prison in the U.S. and France. He was an international scam artist who was "highly intelligent," according to Martin.

Martin also brought in an insurance consultant named Larry Brotzge. With his team in place, a meeting was called and held in the Trump Hotel in New York. As the team of so-called experts drank twenty-five-year-old single-malt whiskey and ate a dinner prepared by one of New York's finest French chefs, they took turns bragging, trying to impress each other like dogs marking their territory. Corbally told stories about Roy Cohn, the famous red-baiting lawyer. Martin tossed out huge dollar amounts for deals he was involved in. Quinn didn't say anything. He was thinking to himself, Don't try to scam a scammer with a bunch of swagger. It doesn't work.

Later they called Rosse in Greenwich, putting him on speaker phone. Rosse joined the bragging and leg-lifting. "I'm still working," Rosse said. "I have to stay on top of all my trades if I want to keep my numbers up where people expect them to be. Right now I'm earning 18% per year trading T-bonds. And I'm pretty confident I can get twenty — if I remain alert."

"Impressive numbers," said Corbally, who was half drunk and feeling self-satisfied. He looked around the hotel room to see if everyone else was won over. He certainly was. Two things impressed Tom Corbally: money and swagger.

"Look," said Rosse, his voice sounding hollow through the speaker phone, as if he was talking into a plastic cup, "I've been trying to buy insurance companies for years. But it never seems to happen. Everybody tells me they're going to make it happen." He paused for effect. "Go make it happen."

Martin, Corbally, and Quinn tried to make it happen. They hired more experts and went flying off to Europe once a month on the Concorde, at $9,000 per flight. In Europe, they found a reinsurance company for Rosse to buy. It was called Cologne Re. At the same time, Rosse was negotiating for insurance companies in Colorado and Washington. All of the purchases would be made with money from the Saint Francis of Assisi Foundation, of which Father Jake was the president.

Then things started to fall apart.

An attorney named Hugh Alexander was hired by Capitol Life Insurance Company to oversee the sale of the company. This was the small company in Colorado that Rosse was trying to buy. While performing due diligence on the sale, Alexander came across the name of Father Jacobs, listed as the president of the Saint Francis Foundation. His signature was on all the legal documents. When Alexander checked on the priest, no one seemed to know him.

Curious, Alexander called the archdiocese in New York. It knew Father Jacobs but told the attorney that he was a scam artist. This caused Alexander to dig a little deeper. When he checked the bank account of the Saint Francis Foundation, one day there was $50 million in it, the next day it was gone. Then it was back two days later. What was going on?

To alleviate Alexander's worries, Monsignor Emilio Colagiovanni agreed to sign an affidavit verifying that the source of the money at Saint Francis Foundation was the Vatican: "the funds . . . have come from funds of the Holy See that are dedicated to use for investment for charitable purposes." The monsignor signed it. But only after Rosse told him over the phone that the promised $5 million — which so far had failed to appear — would show up as soon as he signed it.

"All you have to do is sign it, Emilio," said Rosse, seated in his trading room in Greenwich. He was opening a bottle of purified water, holding the phone between his chin and shoulder. "This is vital to our plans. If we can't pull this purchase off, there won't be any more money for your foundation. You understand?"

"There is no money now, David, in the Monitor's account," said the monsignor, standing in his small apartment in Rome.

"Yeah," drawled Rosse. "About that — there've been a lot of things to take care of, details to keep track of, and . . . well . . . listen, as soon as I get the affidavit back with your signature, I'll transfer the $5 million. It'll be there tomorrow."

"I believe you, David. If I didn't, I wouldn't sign, would I?" said Colagiovanni. "Because if I didn't sign it, then where would you be?" The question hung in the air like a cloud threatening rain.

Rosse hesitated before answering. "You're right. Without you, we wouldn't be in business."

In Rome, Colagiovanni smiled to himself. "Good. Then we understand each other, my friend?"

"Yes, we do," said Rosse.

Colagiovanni picked up a pen and — with an Italian flourish — signed his name on the paper before him.

"There," he said into the phone. "It is done. I will fax it to you immediately."

"Well done, monsignor," said Rosse, "well done."

Despite the affidavit, Alexander kept asking questions. Mostly, he wanted to know the source of the money. Rosse's "experts" danced around the question, never giving a good answer. Their evasions made Alexander keep asking it. As the minutes passed, Rosse's team became more and more nervous because their lies were so unconvincing. The situation went from embarrassing to humiliating to ridiculous. Finally, Rosse's team packed up and went home. The deal was off. A policy of truth was the one thing the team couldn't cheat.

Meanwhile, Rosse was trying to buy another insurance company, Western United Life Assurance Company, in Spokane, Washington. The company had almost $900 million in assets. Rosse drooled at the thought of all that money in his Swiss accounts.

Father Jake led the negotiation team that traveled to Spokane. They met with Western Life's executives. Father Jake passed around pictures.

"This one's of me with Pope John Paul," he said with a dazzling smile. "And here I am with Mother Teresa, in Calcutta." He glanced at the executives in their dark blue Brooks Brothers suits. "What a dump," he said. "Calcutta, I mean."

Then his cell phone rang. He answered.

John Hackney was part of Father Jake's team. While the priest schmoozed on his cell phone, Hackney started dickering over the asking price for Western Life. He thought their price was $20 million too high.

But before the executives could reply, Father Jake put his cell phone back in his pocket. "That was Walter Cronkite," the priest said.

Everyone looked at him.

Father Jake smiled. "He and I go back a long way. But not as far as Lee and I do."

"Lee?" said Hackney.

"Iacocca. Lee Iacocca," said Father Jake.

His cell phone rang again. After two hours of Father Jake's namedropping and phone calls, nothing had been accomplished. Both sides agreed to another meeting in a month.

Paul Sandifur, the president of Western Life, thought Father Jake was pretty much a rodeo clown. He wondered if the guy was really a priest. So he contacted the Vatican. He wanted to know if the whole thing — the Saint Francis of Assisi Foundation — was sanctioned by the Holy See.

The response he received from the Vatican came from Archbishop Giovanni Batista Re. "No such foundation has the approval of the Holy See or exists in the Vatican."

Sandifur immediately called Rosse in Greenwich.

"What the hell is going on?" said Sandifur after reading the Vatican's reply to Rosse.

"It's not a problem," said Rosse, taking a sip of purified water. "Look. Everyone knows how secretive the Vatican is about finances. They don't want anyone to know how much money they have or what they're doing with it. The best thing for you to do is go to Rome and meet with the Saint Francis people face to face."

"I don't think so," said Sandifur. "And until you provide clarification of this matter, this deal isn't going anywhere."

When Rosse got off the phone, he began yelling and screaming. After venting his frustration for thirty minutes, he called Bolan and Colagiovanni. He told them to get to Greenwich as soon as possible. Both men boarded airplanes soon after.

When Colagiovanni entered the trading room in Greenwich, he was annoyed. He still hadn't received the promised $5 million. He had done his part, but Rosse had not fulfilled his part of the bargain.

Bolan was aware of all this but not concerned. He thought it could all be smoothed over. In fact, he was going to suggest that he and Colagiovanni visit the Vatican to do just that. He also intended to recommend that Rosse give the $5 million to Colagiovanni, even though he thought the monsignor was a greedy, conniving, little jerk.

No one would admit what actually took place in the trading room at that meeting. But when it was over, Colagiovanni and Bolan flew to Rome, where they would meet with princes of the Church.

The other thing that left the trading room that day was another affidavit. It was signed by Monsignor Colagiovanni. A copy of it was immediately sent to Paul Sandifur at Western Life. It read, "I hereby certify and confirm to you that Monitor Ecclesiasticus Foundation is the grantor of funds to The Saint Francis of Assisi Foundation. MEF has contributed approximately $1 billion to The Saint Francis Foundation since the creation of the foundation in August 1998." Obviously, Rosse had charmed Colagiovanni right out of his cassock or promised him something in return. Or both.

There was no $1 billion — the number was a big, fat lie. However, on the strength of the affidavit, Sandifur and his Western Life executives flew to Rome, where they met with Monsignor Colagiovanni, who, in turn, charmed them. The insurance executives fell under the spell of the priest's piety, Rome's ancient beauty, and the nearness of the Vatican and its halo of soft persuasion. The meeting was successful, and negotiations began once more.

At almost the same time, Bolan and Colagiovanni huddled with Archbishop Agostino Cacciavillan, who oversaw the Vatican's investments. The archbishop didn't really care what the Saint Francis Foundation did with its money. He insisted only on one thing: that it not identify itself as a Vatican organization.

Too late, though. When Colagiovanni had signed the second affidavit, he had done just that. Conveniently, he had neglected to tell the archbishop.

With a new year — 1999 — came new problems. Insurance commissions in Mississippi and Tennessee began taking a close look at the five insurance companies that Marty Frankel/David Rosse owned in the two states. It was against policy for insurance companies to be owned and operated by an entity outside the state in which they were located. Frankel lived in Greenwich, a long way from Mississippi and Tennessee. As the commissioners examined his companies, they discovered other irregularities. Most glaring was the fact that there appeared to be only $60,000 in an account that supposedly had $69,000,000.

If any of these violations turned out to be true, in the states of Mississippi and Tennessee the penalty was an "automatic felony." It was all true. Not to mention the tiny hiccups of embezzlement, fraud, and falsifying financial documents.

Frankel realized he needed a personal insurance policy against his insurance companies. He felt like Humpty Dumpty — about to take a great fall. When he did, he knew his Swiss bank accounts would be seized, making that money unavailable. So he concocted Plan B — a way to secure large amounts of money outside the United States. It had to be untraceable.

After mulling it over, Frankel decided to give $13 million

to Thomas Quinn, the felonious associate of Corbally. Supposedly, Quinn would hold the funds in offshore accounts, then give them back to Marty when asked. For a percentage, of course — Quinn didn't do anything for free. Frankel wired the money to Quinn's various accounts. Each account was offshore and identified only by numbers.

Within a few days of giving Quinn the money, Frankel changed his mind because of his paranoia. He didn't trust Quinn. He was afraid Quinn wouldn't return the money when he needed it. And he was right. When Quinn was told to return the money, he exploded in anger. "I'm going to come in with a baseball bat and bash your fucking head in, you little nerd," Quinn bellowed at Frankel over the phone.

Frankel, infected by fear, hung up the phone and called Corbally, begging him to do something to protect him. Corbally called Quinn and defused the situation. A few days later Quinn transferred $7 million back to Frankel. He kept the other $6 million as "his fee."

Frankel then switched to Plan C, which meant avoiding trusting anyone but himself with his money. He was going to haul it with him when he fled. He bought $16 million in gold coins from a gold dealer in California, and he worked out a way to buy $10 million worth of diamonds.

To flee undetected with his wealth, Frankel would need a new identity. Again, it had to be untraceable. So he bought a phony birth certificate and a fake passport. These fake documents cost him more than $500,000, yet they were lousy fakes. Anyone — except the one person relying on them — could tell they were forgeries.

On the sly, Frankel also began researching which foreign countries did not have extradition treaties with the United States. He wanted someplace that would not send him back to the U.S. There was no way he wanted to come back and face the charges.

Father Jake and Monsignor Colagiovanni were being set up as the fall guys.

Meanwhile, the insurance commissions in Mississippi and Tennessee made a startling discovery: the five insurance companies were owned by the Saint Francis of Assisi Foundation — located in Rome. The foundation, the commissions learned, was controlled by a Father Peter Jacobs and Monsignor Emilio Colagiovanni. When the commissions investigated, they were informed that Father Jacobs had been "defrocked."

By this point, the commissions had had enough. They contacted John Hackney, Frankel's front man for his insurance empire, and demanded a meeting with Father Jacobs and Monsignor Colagiovanni. The commissions wanted to know what the hell was going on.

The meeting was scheduled for April 29, 1999. Frankel's team flew to Jackson, Mississippi, on a private jet chartered by Frankel/Rosse. The team consisted of Marty Frankel, Tom Bolan, Father Jake, Monsignor Colagiovanni, and John Hackney. They carried with them a forged document affirming that the Monitor Ecclesiasticus Foundation had contributed $1.25 billion to the Saint Francis of Assisi Foundation. This forged piece of paper was supposed to satisfy the commissions.

The team's reasoning was this: if the foundation had that kind of money, along with two saintly priests and the backing of the Vatican, it must be okay. Two of those three things, though, were out-and-out lies. They did not have the backing of the Vatican. And they did not have $1.25 billion. All they had were two priests. Both of whom were con artists.

About six hours before the scheduled meeting, Frankel admitted the truth of the matter to himself. There was no way the commissions would buy it. So Marty went back to his hotel suite, paid his bill, and flew back to Greenwich. He abandoned his "team" to attend the meeting, answer questions, and take the heat. The meeting began without Frankel.

After introductions were made, Monsignor Colagiovanni held his hand out so everyone could see it. On one of his fingers was a large gold ring with a blood-red ruby. "My friends," said Colagiovanni, "His Holiness Pope John Paul II gave me this ring. A token of his esteem."

The commissioner and his lawyers were all Baptists. They stared uneasily at the priest, then glanced at the ring.

Colagiovanni turned to the commissioner, holding his hand up to the man's face. "Would you like to kiss it?" said Colagiovanni.

The commissioner was shocked by the very idea. "Not particularly," he said.

Father Jake said, "It's a beautiful ring. I wish I had one like it." Standing up, he took Colagiovanni's hand and peered closely at the ring. "I had to cancel my lunch with Jimmy Carter to come to this meeting," said Father Jake, sitting back down. "We were going to discuss raising funds to help the needy here in the deep South."

He looked around the room to see if everyone was duly impressed. The Baptists wore puzzled expressions, as if he had just told them he was a Martian.

The commissioner seized the opportunity to change the subject. "Where did the Saint Francis Foundation get all its money?" he asked.

"From the Monitor Ecclesiasticus Foundation," said

Colagiovanni. He placed the forged document on the table in front of the commissioner.

The meeting went downhill from there. Finally, after two hours of getting mumbo-jumbo answers to his questions, the commissioner stopped the meeting. They were getting nowhere. The state of Mississippi would file papers to take over the insurance companies owned by Frankel/Rosse and the foundation. "Once that takes place," said the commissioner, "an intensive investigation will occur. Based on that investigation, criminal charges may or may not be filed." He walked out of the room with his attorneys in tow.

Before the door to the room closed, John Hackney took out his cell phone and hit speed dial. When he got Frankel on the phone, he hissed out what had just taken place. Hackney was scared.

"Relax," Frankel said. "Our attorneys will handle it. It can be smoothed over." He took a sip of bottled water. "Tell everyone to go home. I'll get together with the attorneys, and we'll regroup." Frankel hung up.

Hackney stood dumbfounded, staring at his cell phone, as if it might tell him what to do. Then he shook his head to clear away the confusion. Everything was going to hell, and Frankel was telling him to relax.

In Greenwich, Marty Frankel could see the writing on the wall. Grand jury indictments delivered by the FBI would be arriving soon. He needed to get out of the country as fast as possible. Frankel was packing his bags to leave. Except he had a problem — he had no bags to pack. So he sent his girls out to buy luggage. They returned with fifteen pieces of identical luggage. Enough for Frankel and the two girls he planned to take with him.

He wanted to go somewhere — to some foreign country — that would not throw him out simply because he was charged with a few crimes. But the countries that met that guideline were sorely lacking in every other area of interest to him. As far as Frankel was concerned, most of them were backward, Third World nations, where no one spoke English and where people thought goods and services were automatic weapons and murder-for-hire. Not to mention dirty and breeding grounds for diseases not even named yet. Frankel couldn't spend one night in such places, much less live there for who knew how long. No way.

So he decided on Italy, trusting that all the money he'd paid Fausto Fausti — so far around $1 million — and the man's greed for more money would buy shelter and protection.

Money worried Marty most of all. He would need a lot of it to keep living high. He began making hasty money transfers between his accounts. He had so many accounts that sometimes he couldn't keep them all straight.

Time was running out. There was too much to do! Panic was one breath away. To calm himself and organize his thinking, Frankel wrote "to do" lists on sheets of paper: "launder money," "get $ to Israel, get it back in," "buy fifteen of each of the Notes and Bonds listed on the following two pages. Then I need to sell twelve of each and then buy twelve back."

He moved $600,000 to a bank in Chicago — his hedge account. It was to be used only for legal fees that *might* occur.

On May 4, 1999, five days later, Frankel was ready to leave. He feared it might already be too late. As he walked out the door of his Greenwich mansion, he told his girls to "shred all the documents in the trading room. All of them," he emphasized, sweat on his forehead. "Don't miss any."

"Where are you going, Marty?" asked one of the girls. She had no clue what was going on.

"On a vacation," Frankel snapped.

"Well, when are you coming back?"

"Not for quite a while," he said, trying to slow his breathing. "I need a long vacation."

Outside Marty supervised the loading of his bags in his limousine. Glancing around, he took in all the luxury cars he owned. Rushing back into the mansion, he said, "Anyone who wants one of the cars, take it. Be sure you put the title in your name as soon as possible." Then he went back outside and climbed into his limo, which took him to the White Plains airport, where a chartered Gulfstream sat waiting. Inside the limo with Frankel were $3 million worth of diamonds.

After landing in Spain to refuel, the Gulfstream finally arrived in Rome, where Fausto Fausti waited. Fausti took Frankel and his two girls to the small apartment that would be their hideout. Frankel hated it the second he walked in. It was cheap, dirty, and smelled faintly of human sweat.

Turning to Fausto, Frankel said, "It's a dump."

For the moment, though, it would have to do. Frankel needed to make sure he had plenty of money on hand. So he moved $1.7 million to an account in Germany. Then he sent two of Fausti's henchmen to pick up $300,000 in cash from his account in Switzerland.

Meanwhile, back in Greenwich, everything was going to hell. Rather than shred the documents in Marty's trading room, the girls who had stayed behind had decided it would be faster and easier to burn them. This didn't work. A fire started in the trading room, and soon the flames were licking into the rest of the mansion. An alarm went off. The fire department showed up. After putting out the flames, they started asking questions and became suspicious. The local police were called. When they arrived, they took a look around and became very suspicious. They called the FBI.

In Rome, Frankel moved $454,000 into an Italian bank account, Mona's. Mona had accompanied him to Rome. Through Fausti, Frankel purchased an Italian company called Nuzzaci for $28 million. He paid for it by moving money from his Swiss bank account. But he wasn't really buying a company — he just said he was. What he was really doing was parking his money. This was the deal: he would buy the company but later back out. Most of the $28 million — except for a penalty fee — would be refunded. And conveniently laundered.

On May 16, 1999, a federal judge issued a warrant for Frankel's arrest for wire fraud and money laundering. Many more charges would be added as time went by. The FBI began looking for Frankel and seized his Swiss bank account. He would soon discover that the money in it was no longer available.

FBI agents also wanted to talk with Tom Corbally, his pal Tom Quinn, and Father Peter Jacobs. When Tom Bolan read about the fire in the Greenwich mansion in the newspaper, he hired a good attorney. Bolan knew what was coming.

Back in Rome, both of Marty's girls — Jackie and Mona — were sick of the apartment, which had only two bedrooms and one bathroom. They were used to the lux life: housekeepers, chefs, designer clothes, and chauffeur-driven cars.

"This sucks," said Jackie, standing in her bra and panties. "I'm leaving, and I want some money, Marty."

"Me too," chimed Mona.

"Hey," Frankel said, holding his hands out, trying to calm them down. "You don't want to do that." He glanced around the room, thinking fast. "Look, look," he said. "We'll move to a nice hotel. And do some sightseeing — you know, plan some day trips. You can shop." He gazed at them hopefully.

Jackie shook her head and gestured at the room. "It sucks, Marty. I'm gone." She walked into the bedroom.

"Me too," said Mona.

Frankel gave them each $20,000. Jackie flew back to Greenwich. Mona went to Paris and did some shopping to ease her tension. Then she boarded a flight to New York City, where she contacted a criminal defense attorney. Like Bolan, she knew what was coming.

The FBI arrested her the next day. They put her in a holding cell and left her alone. Later, when they let her out for questioning, she told them everything she knew. Where Marty was in Italy. The money transfers he had made. Everything.

Tom Corbally — good Catholic that he was — decided to adopt the Jesuit philosophy "that the end justifies the means." His end was to avoid jail. His means was to get out of town. He flew to London, where he took an opulent suite at Claridge's Hotel. Where the FBI found him. They didn't have a warrant — yet. They just wanted to ask some questions. Corbally refused to answer. He had a new plan. He would find out where Marty was, then turn him in.

Corbally called Fausti, who put him in touch with Frankel. Frankel told Corbally he was leaving Rome and going to Paris, although in reality he was going to Germany. He guessed Corbally would try to set him up.

Meanwhile, Tom Quinn was trying to locate Frankel. Only Quinn wanted to kill him, not turn him in. In fact, Quinn was ready, willing, and able to kill anyone who could even remotely connect him with Marty. To that end, Quinn had called some pals of his connected to the mafia. Thick, tough-looking men in pin-striped suits started looking for Marty.

The Hotel Prem sat on Lake Alster, a gray expanse of water in Hamburg, Germany. Frankel registered under the name of Roger Ellis and rode the elevator up to his suite. He carried one black suitcase. In the suitcase was $400,000 in cash. His suite was pink.

On September 4, 1999, the FBI asked the local police in Hamburg to arrest Frankel. The FBI gave the police Frankel's suite number at the Hotel Prem. They also provided the police with a photo of Marty. The black-and-white photo showed a skinny, geeky-looking guy with thick glasses. The Hamburg police laughed at the picture. The guy certainly didn't look like a criminal genius.

Arriving at the Hotel Prem, a squad of policemen rode the elevator up to the fifth floor. They didn't knock or kick it in. They used a pass-key the manager of the hotel had given them.

Frankel froze like a statue as the police walked in. Realization sank in. His eyes, huge behind his thick glasses, filled with tears. He took one step forward. "You got me," he said.

The police handcuffed him and gathered up all his personal belongings. One of the policemen picked up his black suitcase, hefted it, and laughed. He said something in

German to the others, who smiled and chuckled.

At the police station, Frankel sat in a medium-sized room, an office of some sort. It was not a holding cell. Fear threatened to suck him into another world. His senses flicked in and out of reality, as if he was in the *Twilight Zone*, as Frankel later described his experience to a German newspaper reporter.

Two policemen entered the room. Tall and Teutonic looking, short blond hair and blue eyes. The last one through carefully shut the door. They both wore suits. Both spoke English remarkably well. Later Marty found out they were lieutenant inspectors.

"You are Martin Frankel?"

"Yes, yes, yes," said Marty. Panic took over his face. "Look. There are people trying to kill me. Mafia mob people. If you send me back to America, they will kill me, and you'll be responsible for my death."

The two policemen glanced at each other. One of them rolled his eyes. His partner gave a small nod.

"We have nothing to do with extradition," said one of the policemen. "That is an issue outside our authority. We just want to ask you some questions regarding your passport." He looked down at Marty, who sat behind a table.

He did not seem to listen or understand. "I know things," Frankel said. "I have vital information about Massimo D'Alema. He is connected." Frankel scrunched up his eyes and leered. Massimo D'Alema was the prime minister of Italy. "The mafia tell him what to do," Frankel gushed. "He and the mafia are lying in the same bed. Yeltsin doesn't want the pope to visit, but I'll send my people to persuade him. Vernon Jordan could do it. If Clinton would let him. Then the old Boris Yeltsin would have to give in. But no, not him.

Has to have his own way all the time."

The lieutenant inspectors looked at each other. One of them shrugged, making a what-the-hell-is-he-talking-about face. With his eyes wide beneath upraised eyebrows, his partner shook his head.

"Herr Frankel," he said in a soft voice. "You are not making sense. Perhaps we can get you something to drink? Then you will feel better, huh?"

"Yes, yes, yes," muttered Marty. "The mafia's in bed with all of them. Yeltsin and Quinn — if I go back, they'll kill me. The pope wants to go to Russia, but I can't allow it."

"Excuse us, *bitte*, Herr Frankel," said one of the policemen politely. He motioned his partner outside.

In the hallway, the two inspectors discussed the nutcase in the other room. Perhaps he was mentally deficient or on drugs. Or maybe he wanted to make a deal — a plea bargain. They couldn't decide. They did decide to contact an attorney for him. If they violated his rights, he'd walk, and they'd be embarrassed.

One of them pulled out his cell phone to call an attorney. The other went back into the room, where Frankel was still rambling on.

Thirty minutes later Thomas Piplak entered the room. He was a criminal defence attorney. The two inspectors stood in the room with their arms crossed, listening to Frankel, who had not stopped babbling.

"Herr Frankel," said the attorney, "I am Thomas Piplak. I have been asked to take your case."

Marty mumbled something about the pope and the mafia.

"Herr Frankel," said Piplak. "For your own sake, you must stop talking."

Marty stopped and looked up at Piplak. "What?"

"It is not in your best interest to make any comments in front of the police," said Piplak, indicating the two inspectors. "You need to say nothing. Is that clear?"

Marty thought about that. Then nodded.

Traveling with a false passport — that's all the Hamburg police charged Marty with. All the rest — the money laundering, fraud, forgery, wire transfers — was for the Americans to deal with.

But then things changed. The police examined the bag they had found in Marty's room at the Hotel Prem. Inside they discovered 814 diamonds, $400,000 in cash, and a laptop computer. One of the diamonds was round-cut, 15.67 carats. The bag also contained twelve passports, each with a photo of Marty, each with a different name.

The Hamburg police suspected that the diamonds had been stolen but couldn't prove it. In reality, they hadn't been stolen. But they had been purchased with embezzled money.

Marty soon found himself in a German jail. The charges were traveling with a false passport, failing to pay taxes on diamonds when he entered Germany, and smuggling diamonds.

Piplak did what he could for Marty. In the end, Marty was sentenced to three years in a German prison. Which was just fine by him. He didn't mind three years in prison. What he did not want was to be sent back to the U.S., which had begun the extradition process.

Meanwhile, Marty Frankel felt as if he had gone to hell. German prisons were different from U.S. prisons. The latter were rated as Club Meds, as Frankel would later learn when he was extradited.

The Germans put him in the Untersuchungshaftanstalt prison, called UHA for short. UHA was a gray block of cement on Holstenglacis Street. Dreary didn't begin to describe it.

Marty had bread and water for breakfast. For lunch he received a bowl of plain white rice and one cup of coffee. Dinner was more bread and water.

Marty wrote letters to friends and family in the United States, begging them for money so that he could buy canned tuna and crackers from the prison commissary. Fortunately, a few people did not turn their backs on him. Otherwise, as he said, "I would have starved to death."

Piplak fought extradition, mostly by stalling. But he knew he couldn't win.

Meanwhile, all Marty's accomplices made deals with the federal prosecutors. On the advice of their attorneys, Corbally and his pal Larry Martin refused to answer any and all questions. They hadn't been charged, and until they were they weren't talking. Most of Marty's "girls" made deals or pled guilty to money laundering. John Hackney admitted he broke the law but claimed ignorance as his excuse. He did not know that Marty was embezzling insurance funds. In the end, he pled guilty to money laundering and conspiracy charges. It was either that or go to trial. If he lost the trial — which he undoubtedly would — he would spend the next twenty years in prison.

In March 2001, a Lufthansa airliner landed in New York City. Marty Frankel sat on the plane — in the economy section. How humiliating. Plastic handcuffs hugged his wrists. Federal marshals sat on either side of him.

Marty and his escorts waited until everyone else had left the plane. As the three men walked into the concourse, dozens of heavily armed policemen greeted them. Outside the airport, a police helicopter hovered overhead.

The police loaded Frankel into an suv and drove him to

Connecticut, where he was tossed into a holding cell. His glasses were taken from him. The lights in his cell burned brightly twenty-four hours a day. A few months later he was transferred to a jail in Suffield, Connecticut, where he awaited his trial. Since he had no money, Marty found himself saddled with a public defender.

Public defenders were overworked, underpaid, and didn't have time to care. Besides, they were "officers of the court." Which meant their loyalties — ultimately — rested with the source of their measly paychecks. Marty knew he was on his way to hell.

While he languished, in August 2001 Monsignor Emilio Colagiovanni flew to Cleveland to visit family. One of his sisters was old and ill, and another sister had just died. As he prepared to say mass for his dead sister, two men seated in the back of the church rose and walked forward. Colagiovanni glared at them. Sacrilege! One of the men pulled out a leather wallet with a badge in it. FBI agents. They cuffed him, read him his rights, and led him away to a waiting SUV.

Two federal marshals met Colagiovanni at the Cleveland airport. They escorted him onto a plane, which flew to Connecticut. He was placed in a holding tank. The next morning he was arraigned before a federal judge. Since he was a priest and not deemed a flight risk, he was allowed to post bail. But he couldn't leave the U.S.

Monsignor Colagiovanni was eighty-one — an old man. And he was angry and bitter. The promised $5 million had never shown up. A pittance — $40,000 was all he had to show for his work on Frankel/Rosse's behalf. His reputation was ruined. He wanted to see others — Vatican officials — get their comeuppance. They were as guilty as he was.

Colagiovanni hired a leading criminal defence attorney, a

good Catholic, who began negotiating a deal with the federal prosecutors. Colagiovanni was confident the feds would deal.

"My friend," he told his attorney, "no one — not even the government — wants to rise up against the Church. For to do so presents them as persecutors. A public relations nightmare."

The attorney agreed. "You're right. They'll probably go for a fine and a slap on the hand. But you'll have to give them something in return, you know?" He peered over the tops of his glasses at the monsignor.

Colagiovanni sat in a leather chair, his hands clasped on his stomach. He nodded. Then a naughty smile caught at his lips. "My friend," he said in a quiet voice, "I am counting on it."

Looking at Colagiovanni, the attorney knew what people meant when they said "like swimming with sharks." He reminded himself to stay out of the water.

One year later, on September 6, 2002, Colagiovanni stood in Federal District Court in New Haven, Connecticut. Seated before him was Judge Ellen Bree Burns. In front of Judge Burns was a six-page plea statement. In it, Colagiovanni pled guilty to conspiracy to commit wire fraud and launder money. He also named Monsignor Francis Salerno and Archbishop Giovanni Battista Re in the plea statement. And he agreed to cooperate with federal authorities in their investigation of the case. Translation: Colagiovanni agreed to snitch on everyone in the scheme, telling the feds everything he knew.

He was now eighty-two. Before the deal, he was looking at five years in prison and a fine of $250,000. Because he had made the deal and signed the plea statement, he would receive much less punishment. Knowing this, Colagiovanni smiled and relaxed.

Judge Burns told him to return three months later for a status hearing and probable sentencing. Colagiovanni nodded, smiled, and said, "Thank you, Judge." Then he turned and walked out with his attorney. Outside a light breeze ruffled his comb-over. He patted his hair back into place and went to buy a coffee at Starbucks. He had recently developed a taste for lattes.

On December 9, 2002, Monsignor Emilio Giovanni received his sentence from Judge Burns. A fine of $15,000.

Colagiovanni smiled. The shadow of the Church protected the faithful.

At a table in the court, Colagiovanni signed a copy of his court papers in front of a bailiff, who tore off the pink copy and handed it to the priest. Colagiovanni folded it and tucked it under his red cincture, the religious sash around his waist. Checking his hair, he gave it a pat. Then he walked out, looking straight ahead.

When Father Jake read about Martin Frankel/David Rosse in the newspapers, he was sitting at his favorite table at his favorite sidewalk café in Rome. Here he people-watched and read the newspapers. His blue Vespa balanced on its kickstand ten yards away. As he scanned the article, he knew he would be implicated.

Setting the paper down, he took a sip of espresso and thought about being implicated. Then he shrugged. He wouldn't let it worry him. If they wanted to question him, he was easy to find. Until then, he would enjoy life as he had always done — his way.

Besides, he was seventy-six. There wasn't much they could do to him. And as he had learned through experience, a priest in the Church is viewed as special, almost untouchable.

Father Jake paid his bill and strolled over to his Vespa. Pulling up the dress of his black cassock, he tucked it into his sash. Swinging a leg over, he straddled the scooter and turned the key. The familiar brupping sound was music to his ears. He twisted the throttle and shot out into traffic. It was a little like flying, he thought.

Three weeks later he received a summons from Archbishop Battista Re, who sat behind his ornate white desk on a red velvet chair. Sunlight flowed through the south windows of the office, quickening the gold rings on the archbishop's hands. The rings glowed like droplets from a fireball.

"My dear Father Jake," said the archbishop, standing and holding out his hand.

"Your Grace," Father Jake said, kissing the biggest ring on the hand.

"Please, dear friend, be seated." The archbishop waved at another red velvet chair.

As Father Jake sat down, the archbishop came right to the point. "You have read, have you not, my dear Father Jake, of the plague of troubles visiting Monsignor Colagiovanni and his . . ." — he paused, carefully choosing a word — ". . . associates?"

"Yes, I have, Your Grace," said Father Jake, smiling. Emilio's predicament amused him.

"And what opinion have you formed about all of this?" asked the archbishop, making a grand gesture with his hands, as if he was catching a giant beach ball.

Father Jake thought for a moment. "Well, I feel somewhat responsible for Emilio's predicament. And a little embarrassed by my foolishness in allowing myself to be hoodwinked by dishonest men," he said. "But then I've never had a head for business matters, as anyone will tell you. I am easily fooled."

91

The archbishop nodded. "Aren't we all, my dear friend? Aren't we all?" He toyed with one of the rings on his left hand. A troubled look settled on his face. "I have a great favor to ask of you, my dear Father Jake," he said. "The Holy Mother Church," he waved a hand vaguely in the air, "believes it would be remedial if you were to return to the United States and communicate with the authorities." He leaned forward and spoke softly. "Nothing ruinous, you understand? And the entire body of our Holy Mother Church will stand at your shoulder, comforting and protecting you." Smiling, the archbishop sat back in his chair and waited.

Father Jake understood. According to yesterday's papers, the FBI had a warrant for his arrest. He had just been ordered to turn himself in. And the Church would hire the best attorneys that money could buy to defend him. The Vatican wanted the situation to vanish.

Father Jake said, "I understand, Your Grace. I will make preparations to leave immediately."

Archbishop Battista Re nodded. "Thank you, my dear friend Father Jake. I will say a prayer." The archbishop stood and held out his hand to be kissed. The meeting was over.

Father Peter Jacobs flew back to the United States, where he turned himself in to the federal court. His attorneys were with him. The judge released Father Jake on his own recognizance. Immediately, his attorneys began negotiating a deal with federal prosecutors.

Father Jake had received $18,000 in cash from "David Rosse," along with first-class airline tickets, luxury hotel suites, and premium foods and beverages. He had been given a Volkswagen automobile as an incentive, which in reality was a hush payment. He had misrepresented Walter Cronkite and Lee Iacocca as directors of the Saint Francis of Assisi Foundation.

Father Jake knew that Rosse would donate $55 million to the Monitor Ecclesiasticus Foundation but then withdraw and control all but $5 million of the "washed" money. This maneuver was to be secret, as was Rosse's link to the money and the foundation. Father Jake tacitly agreed to this scheme. As president of the Saint Francis of Assisi Foundation, he misrepresented the source and amount of its funds. In other words, Father Jake deliberately and knowingly lied.

He also signed a legal document stating that the MEF had given $1.5 billion to the Saint Francis of Assisi Foundation. This, too, was a lie, and Father Jake knew he was lying when he signed the document.

He introduced Rosse to Monsignor Colagiovanni. And then Father Jake accompanied Thomas Bolan to the Vatican, where he introduced Bolan to high-ranking officials of the Holy See. He tried to ease negotiations between Bolan and the Vatican so that a charity could be set up. This charity would be a front for criminal activities: fraud, embezzlement, and money laundering.

He also made false statements to the Mississippi insurance commission.

Father Jake did all of this knowingly and of his own free will.

Yet in court, standing before Judge Burns, Father Jake's attorneys claimed that their client — a Roman Catholic priest — had merely "been trying to help Mr. Rosse help others less fortunate. Father Jacobs had no knowledge of the precise purpose of Mr. Rosse's charitable inclinations."

Judge Burns scowled down from her bench.

"Anyone who knows Father Jacobs," said one of his

attorneys, placing a hand on the priest's shoulder, "knows that it is completely conceivable that — because of his trusting nature — he could be fooled by evil people." The attorney glanced at the judge to see if she was buying his spiel.

Judge Burns spoke to Father Jake. "What do you have to say, Father? Is it true that you did not realize — or even guess — what was going on here?"

Father Jake tilted his head and smiled at the judge. "Your Honor, Cardinal Spellman once said to me that 'Priests in business either fool people or get fooled.' To my dismay, Your Honor, I was fooled."

Judge Burns gazed at him intently, as if reading very small print. Then she said, "Hmmm," and nodded tightly.

In the end, on October 13, 2004, seventy-eight-year-old Father Peter Jacobs was sentenced to a five-year term of probation. A slap on the wrist.

Interviewed shortly after his sentencing, he spoke about his friendly feelings toward Rosse/Frankel. The interview took place at a local coffee shop. Pastel yellow Italian tiles patterned the floor. Outside gray skies looked down at the city of New Haven.

"People who worked for him said I was the only one who gave him peace," Father Jake said. "I may have been kind of a psychiatrist for David. If he winds up in prison, I would certainly go and try to help him. As a priest, I can't let him down."

When asked about the Church's reaction to the scandal, Father Jake smiled, took a sip of his coffee, and said, "Priests can be very uncharitable toward one another." Then he pushed a letter across the table to the interviewer, who was from a major magazine. "That's a letter from Pope Paul VI," he gushed. "Written by his private secretary, dictated by the pope himself." Leaning forward, he pointed at the letter. "Pope Paul praises me for my work performing mixed marriages."

"But I thought the Church invalidated the marriages you had performed? Any since 1983?" said the interviewer.

"They are disputed," corrected Father Jake. "But this letter confirms them all — from the highest level in the Holy Church." He shook his head sadly. "It's the same thing as when I opened my restaurant. All the proceeds went to charity. A friend of mine — a bishop from Harlem — helped me get my liquor license." He looked around the coffee shop, then out the window. "Some powerful people didn't like it. The media coverage and all." He smiled at the interviewer. "Priests can become jealous too." He sighed. "We are only human."

The Vatican denied any connection to the Monitor Ecclesiasticus Foundation. Indeed, Bishop Salerno told *Fortune* magazine that "I don't know who Bolan is" and that he never received any letters or communications of any type from Thomas Bolan. The Church was trying to distance itself from the whole scandalous affair. They kept scraping the mud off their boots, but there was no mud to begin with.

Today Father Jake is off probation, living in Rome, tooling around on his blue Vespa — a new model. He travels widely, giving spiritual advice, performing mixed marriages, and saying mass. He still does as he pleases.

Father Jake doesn't feel as if he did anything wrong. In his opinion, he's not going to hell.

On December 11, 2004, Martin Frankel, aka David Rosse, was led into Federal Court by two bailiffs. His hair had been cut short, and he had shaved his scraggly beard for his appearance in court. That day he would be sentenced. He sat in a brown leather chair.

His court-appointed attorney was on his feet, arguing about the amount of money his client had embezzled. "I disagree with the prosecutor's figure of $200 million," said Bill Koch. "I think the figure is much, much lower than that, Your Honor."

Judge Burns said, "What is your estimate, counselor?"

"Less than $80 million," said Koch. He picked up a sheet of paper from the table and glanced at it. "Around $66 to 68 million."

Judge Burns allowed a small smile to touch her mouth. She knew, as did Koch, that that figure was low. She also knew why he had said $80 million — because federal sentencing guidelines demanded very stiff penalties for any amount over $80 million. Koch was simply trying to reduce his client's time in prison. She didn't blame him for that. It was his job to do so.

The U.S. prosecuting attorney, Kevin O'Connor, had presented evidence that Frankel had siphoned off a minimum of $200 million from insurance companies.

"The court will go with the $200 million figure, counselor," said Judge Burns.

The ruling did not appear to surprise Koch, who simply nodded.

Marty Frankel sat listening attentively, making notes on a tablet in front of him.

They had tried every ploy they could think of to gain the judge's sympathy. First, they had declared that Marty had a mental disorder and didn't know right from wrong. In other words, he was insane — in a harmless way. Then they had informed the judge that all of his friends had deserted him. He had no one. That didn't work either. So they had asked the judge to give Marty a break because of the harsh, cruel, and archaic conditions of the German prison he had been in. The judge was not impressed.

So far the only thing going in Marty's favor was that the federal prosecutor had told the judge that Marty had cooperated in "recovering assets and pursuing his accomplices."

Marty was in deep shit.

The judge looked at him and said, "Mr. Frankel, before I sentence you, do you have anything you wish to say?"

Marty rose. "I want to apologize to everybody," he said. "The last thing I wanted to have happen to my insurance companies was to have them go under." He glanced around the courtroom nervously. Then he took off on a forty-minute rambling speech in which he bounced from subject to subject. It was totally disjointed, almost incoherent, and everyone who heard it came to the conclusion that Marty was an interesting madman. He quoted the Bible, sprinkling in verses about forgiveness, tolerance, and love for fellow believers who had failed. In between his preaching episodes, he bad-mouthed his former associates and told a few lame jokes. He finished with a plea for leniency, begging the judge to have pity and shower mercy on him.

"Most everything I did was because of a woman, Your Honor. For Sonia Howe — the love of my life. I just wanted enough money to protect her and her two darling children — who I think of as my own — from harm."

Frankel had met Howe years ago. She became his mistress for a while and knew about his schemes. After a while, she got tired of Frankel and left, taking a lot of money and moving to Europe. For some bizarre reason, he resurrected her in his mind as his soulmate, whom he was caring for.

Howe remembered Frankel as "a geeky-looking guy I lived with for a while." She had almost completely forgotten him.

Judge Burns pinched her face in disbelief. "So you stole $209 million in order to take care of the children?" she asked.

"No," said Marty. "Can I explain it to you?"

"I'm begging you to explain it to me," Judge Burns said.

"Well, Your Honor, once I got going on it — you understand — on falsifying financial statements, the whole thing would have come apart if I just stopped. So I really had no choice. I had to keep going and hope that I could make enough money to pay back my insurance companies."

Judge Burns put her fingers to her forehead, as if she had a headache.

Bill Koch rolled his eyes at the ceiling.

"For that reason — I'm asking you to show me some compassion. Because punishment for the sake of deterrence does not work for someone who does not know the difference between right and wrong," said Marty. "If somebody is mentally ill, you shouldn't punish them, because it won't stop other mentally ill people from doing it." Marty sat down.

Senior Judge Ellen Bree Burns of Federal District Court sentenced Martin R. Frankel to sixteen years, eight months, in prison.

Marty was fifty years old. He will be eligible for parole when he is sixty-one, in 2015. At this time, he is in the minimum-security Federal Correction Institute in Big Springs, Texas.

No one is really sure how much money Marty embezzled.

Estimates place the amount anywhere from $200 million to over $1 billion, with most experts believing it was $335 million. Some people think Marty still has money secreted in bank accounts all over the world.

Thomas Bolan's turn before Judge Burns came on May 24, 2005. His attorney, whose name was Maurice Nessen, had hammered out a deal — a plea bargain — with the prosecutors. The deal went like this: if Bolan would cooperate with the feds' investigation, and if he would plead guilty to one count of misprision of a felony, the feds would advise the judge to let him off easy.

It was one heck of a deal. Especially since Bolan had accepted payments of over $200,000, along with first-class travel expenses all over the world and the use of a chauffeur-driven Mercedes from Rosse/Frankel. In on the scheme from the start, Bolan had negotiated with Vatican officials, prepared bogus documents, and stood by while Monsignor Colagiovanni lied about having given $1.2 billion to the Saint Francis of Assisi Foundation.

When Bolan admitted to misprision of a felony, all he really did was say he had made a mistake — an error in judgment. Misprision of a felony, in law, is when someone knows that a serious crime is taking place but doesn't take part in or assist it. He or she knows about it and, for some reason, doesn't mention it to the police.

More than likely, the feds didn't have enough on Bolan to make a case against him. So at ten o'clock in the morning, in New Haven, on a warm spring day, Judge Burns pronounced sentence on him. "One year of probation and a fine of $10,000."

After he heard the judge's words, Bolan turned to his attorney and smiled. Then the two men shook hands. Bolan, dressed in a $3,000 suit, looked very dapper. Despite the enormous amounts of money he was paying his attorney, he felt good. His business interests were flourishing, the money was rolling in, and as soon as he paid the $10,000 fine this incident would be behind him.

Hell, he was only eighty years old.

Thomas Quinn never came up on charges. His reputation was that he took care of business — in a very lethal way. And even if someone had squealed on him, telling the feds about his part in the scheme, it was doubtful the feds could make any charge stick.

Quinn simply disappeared. He had $6 million of Marty's money and who knows how much from his other enterprises. Most people believe he lives in Europe somewhere, where he lounges by his pool, plotting other schemes to make money.

Thomas Corbally escaped too. But he had to die to do it. On April 15, 2004, he died in New York City. The feds were still trying to make a case against him and probably would have succeeded.

Along with all the first-class Concorde trips he took to Europe and back — which Frankel paid for — and all the costs of luxury hotels, food, and beverages he ran up — which Frankel paid for — Corbally took Marty for the following: a $5.8 million apartment in New York, $1.5 million in a Swiss bank account, a chauffeur-driven Mercedes 600 SL, and $112,000 worth of charges on an American Express credit card.

To quote Aretha Franklin, "Who's zoomin' who?"

Anyone who knew him was not surprised that Corbally was part of such a scheme. He operated in the fast lane his whole life. When he died, Corbally was eighty-three.

# CHAPTER 3

# FATHER FLIM FLAM

THE YEAR WAS 1997. The place was St. John the Martyr Catholic Church, located on East 71st Street — the hoity-toity Upper East Side of New York City.

Eighty-one-year-old Rose Cale arrived at St. John's for mass. Rose had attended mass every day for the past thirteen years. Only not at St. John's. That day marked her first mass at St. John's. She decided to try it out because she had heard wonderful reports of St. John's marvelous pastor — Monsignor John Woolsey.

According to her friends, Woolsey preached with the simple eloquence of his namesake, the Apostle John, "making the mass come alive with vibrancy." That wasn't all either. He was charming, full of energy, and very good looking. Some even used the word *handsome*. More important, he cared deeply about his parishioners and took a personal interest in each and every one.

That was the trait that got Rose.

Like most elderly churchgoing women, Rose desired attention. She was old, lonely, and rich. She'd spent her entire working life as a professional secretary, giving attention to her employers. It was her turn now.

Dissatisfied with her last church and its young, hip priest — who didn't even know her name — and his never-ending rants about abortion and tolerance of homosexuals and world peace, Rose had thought about quitting for more than a year. But daily mass had become her only comfort in old age. She didn't know what to do.

Then she'd heard about Monsignor Woolsey and St. John the Martyr. And she knew God had answered her prayers. So here she was.

Monsignor John Woolsey, tall, deeply tanned, and very fit, was fifty-nine. He looked like Kirk Douglas without the chin dimple.

After taking his theological training at St. Joseph Seminary in Yonkers, he took Holy Orders in 1965. Assigned to St. Margaret of Antioch Parish in Pearl River, New York, he dazzled congregations from day one. His sermons were inspirational without being sickly sweet. In no time at all, St. Margaret's was bulging with members. Some Sunday masses were standing room only. Donations flowed into the church like the Nile River. Everyone felt spiritual, as if they had somehow wandered into a special place. The Archdiocese of New York took notice. Father Woolsey was an up-and-comer, and his grooming for bigger and better things began.

In 1977, Father Woolsey took over as assistant director of the archdiocese's Office of Christian and Family Development. Ten years later he was appointed director.

His boss was Cardinal John O'Connor. Father Woolsey's

job was to coordinate and carry out anti-abortion programs. It wasn't just an office job and sitting behind a big desk telling people what to do. Father Woolsey climbed into the ring and did battle. He made speeches, attended rallies, and shepherded marches through the streets. He also did marriage counseling and parental counseling and taught natural family-planning classes to good Catholics.

Father Woolsey protested against AIDS education in the public schools. And he made stirring speeches against gay rights. He was the perfect priest, carrying the banner of the Holy Mother Church against sin and evil and the devil, the mastermind of both.

The monsignor had one flaw that no one knew about: he liked money and what it could buy. Father Woolsey preferred the chic life. Luxury cars, fine dining, posh vacations, and golf gave more flavoring to life, as far as he was concerned. And upscale watches such as a Rolex added zip to everything.

But posh was out of reach. Father Woolsey made only $15,000 per year, plus fifteen dollars per mass he performed.

In 1996, Father Woolsey — now Monsignor Woolsey — was appointed pastor of St. John the Martyr, and he was made co-vicar of East Manhattan. The title of monsignor meant he was a dignitary of the Roman Catholic Church. And in the Church, "dignitary" was equivalent to being a celebrity. He was a somebody.

Although he wasn't a bishop yet, Monsignor Woolsey was higher than a priest. Technically, he was *vicar forane*: a priest appointed by a bishop to rule over a district. But he shared the responsibility with another, so he was co-vicar, which meant he was now a deputy bishop. He was in the fast lane.

It also meant Monsignor Woolsey was in charge of, and had access to, money.

After mass was over and he'd changed into his house cassock, Monsignor Woolsey mingled with his parishioners in the multi-use room, a large open hall with hardwood floors and a stage at one end. Tables with white cloths held casseroles, salads, chicken, ham, hot dogs, and a colorful array of desserts. Coffee, soft drinks, water, and bottled juices sat nearby.

Monsignor Woolsey poured himself a cup of coffee, then surveyed the room as he took a sip. People stood in small groups, chatting and smiling. Others sat at tables and ate. Still others sat and people-watched.

People-watching was one of his favorite pastimes. It allowed the monsignor to size others up. Movements and facial expressions gave insight into people's fears and worries, while their clothing, posture, and shoes revealed much about their bank accounts. Especially shoes. Over the years, Monsignor Woolsey had discovered that rich people who were stingy and tightfisted skimped on their shoes. They bought cheap shoes. They wore designer clothing that cost thousands yet walked around in stiff, ill-fitting shoes that cost fifty dollars. Their stinginess showed in the offering plate too. They dropped in a few dollars each week and thought they were generous givers, whereas the people who wore quality shoes, which carried a hefty price tag, really were generous. These were the people the monsignor sought out.

There was one now. An elderly woman sat with three other women at one of the tables. She was picking at a fruit salad. Nice shoes adorned her feet. To Monsignor Woolsey, "nice" meant expensive. Hers looked like Manolo's.

Walking toward the four women, Woolsey smiled as he passed through the hall. Everyone smiled back at him. Some waved. They all loved him. He could feel it.

Approaching the table, he held out his arms as if he was

embracing the whole room. His smile beamed, his eyes twinkled with holy friskiness. "Ladies!" he boomed in his full-flavored voice. "How are you on this glorious day?"

Four smiling faces looked up at him. His attention delighted them. After all, most of New York City knew who Monsignor Woolsey was. At least anyone who was anyone, that is.

He took the woman's hand in his, giving it a little squeeze. "I don't recognize you," he said. He gave her his best smile. "Whenever there's a new face, I can't rest until I know who it is. Why they're here and what I can do for them."

Rose Cale blushed. She felt like a teenager. What a very nice man, she almost said out loud.

Monsignor Woolsey patted her hand. "I'm Father John Woolsey," he said.

One of the women turned to Rose. "He's always so modest. Actually, he's Monsignor Woolsey," she said, bestowing majestic force on the word *Monsignor*.

Rose nodded. "Of course, everyone knows who you are, Monsignor," she whispered. "I'm Rose Cale."

"I'm very pleased you're here, Rose," said Monsignor Woolsey, still holding her hand. "I look forward to getting to know you." He laughed. "Now I sound like I'm auditioning for a part in *The King and I*."

The four women laughed.

Monsignor Woolsey leaned closer to the group. "I have to go mingle some more, otherwise someone will feel left out. They'll say I spend all my time with beautiful women," he said in a low voice that bubbled with merriment. He stood straight and winked at them. "So I'll ask you to excuse me."

The four women nodded in unison.

As he walked away, Monsignor Woolsey turned, pointed

at the ceiling, and boomed, "But I'll be back." The famous priest moved off to greet other admirers.

Rose looked at her friends. "What a nice man," she said. "I think I'm going to like it here."

Monsignor Woolsey did come back. And back and back and back. Rose attended mass every day, and every day the priest sought her out afterward. They talked.

Then one day Rose invited the monsignor to lunch with her. He accepted. They both had the Caesar salad with grilled salmon, along with a subtle Chardonnay. And they talked. Before long, they lunched together two or three times a week.

Rose had inherited family money. Monsignor Woolsey listened to her concerns about her stocks. Her brokerage firm was Prudential Securities. Since he did some modest trading too, he gave her sensible advice. One day he recommended his broker to her, that is if she were ever to consider a change. He never pushed. He just submitted ideas for her to think about.

Monsignor Woolsey began taking Rose to her medical appointments, where he sat in the waiting room, reading a magazine, or chatted with the nurses. He charmed them all with his good looks, his smile, his rich voice, and his zest for life.

Cards and letters arrived in Rose's mail. They were from Monsignor Woolsey. Sometimes they had inspirational quotations, other times stock tips he had received from his broker. Mostly, they just expressed his care for her as his friend. They were always signed "Love, Monsignor Woolsey."

Rose was charmed. She sent him thank-you notes. Before she sealed the envelopes, she put a check in each. The checks, payable to St. John the Martyr Church, were sizable donations. She made many of them.

As Easter of 1999 approached, Monsignor Woolsey sent Rose a copy of his Palm Sunday sermon. She got to read it before anyone else heard it. She felt honored to have such a close friend. The sermon was titled "Journeying with Christ."

The primary focus of Palm Sunday is the triumphal entrance of Christ into the city of Jerusalem. Word of Christ's coming was the reason that huge crowds had gathered along the streets to catch a glimpse of the one whose reputation had caught their interest.

The people, we are told, were carrying palms, the traditional sign of welcome to a royal visitor.

As people today line the canyon streets of lower Manhattan to acknowledge our present-day "heroes," these people had come to acknowledge Christ the Savior. In the person of Jesus, the King of Kings, a royal personage was in their midst — indeed salvation was in their midst.

While we naturally look back and reflect upon this exciting day, we must be careful not to linger excessively in historical revelry.

Christ came not just for the people of Jerusalem; he came for us as well. Salvation in the person of Christ is now in our midst. Today, it is our time to venture out with palms in hand to welcome the royal Savior.

Our involvement must not end here. We must not return home and resume "business as usual." On the contrary, we must return to our homes and place our palms in a most prominent place to remind us that our Palm Sunday experience is the beginning of a very holy week — the redemptive journey of Christ.

Yes, we cheer as he enters our midst, but we must continue our journey with him. We must proceed with him to the upper room on Holy Thursday and rejoice in the institution of the Eucharist.

We move along with Mary, Mary of Cleophas, and John to the Mount of Calvary on Good Friday and humbly venerate the redemptive Christ.

And then, with alleluias bursting from our lips, we rejoice on Easter morning. The long spell of death is over — for he has risen.

May this Holy Week renew our efforts to live a holy life filled with hope and joy.

As Rose finished reading it, her breast swelled with emotion. She felt as if the man who wrote these words, and who would speak them in her church, was royalty too, and in turn she was the friend of a royal personage.

Taking up paper and pen, she poured out her thoughts in a note to Monsignor Woolsey. Then she dropped in another sizable check.

When he received the note, he opened his mouth in a silent belly laugh. Then, tearing the envelope open, he took out the check. Smiling, he held it out at arm's length. Ten grand. Perfect. He didn't even unfold the handwritten note, just tore it up and tossed the pieces in a nearby trashcan.

In the past few years, Rose had donated $80,000 to the church. Just as her expensive Manolo shoes had predicted, she was a generous giver. Monsignor Woolsey had pocketed and spent the whole eighty grand. He had purchased a new Lexus. It was tan with a tan leather interior. Then he had bought a gold Breguet watch. Covetousness filled his heart the first time he saw it. He had to have it. Rose Cale's money had made it happen.

With this latest gift of $10,000, the monsignor was considering moving up to a Rolex. Maybe the one with all the diamonds. Or a Breitling — now that was a timepiece. He told the salesman at the jewelry store that he expected to come into a large sum of money in the near future.

Monsignor Woolsey never allowed himself more than one watch at a time. When he lusted for a new one, he traded the old one in on it. The theory behind this thinking was that he didn't want to succumb to greed and end up owning five or ten watches. He could wear only one at a time. Additionally, this way he could enjoy many different brands. If he kept them all, he'd run out of money after about five of them. No, this was a much better way. It made him feel more in control. The other way his desires would control him.

Ever since taking up his position at St. John the Martyr and his appointment as co-vicar, Monsignor Woolsey had skimmed about $100,000 per year from the church. It was easy. He simply opened an additional account at the same bank and deposited the stolen funds in it. The bank certainly wasn't suspicious. How could it be? St. John the Martyr Catholic Church had always banked there, and the church was constantly opening separate accounts for special projects. Besides, he was Monsignor Woolsey, famous and above criticism.

Then he adjusted the figures in the church's financial records. He called it "creative bookkeeping." When the archdiocese asked how he was spending the church's money, he just lied.

Woolsey used the skimmed money to satisfy his larger desires. He explained it to himself this way. People who have a great capacity for life naturally have larger desires. People with little capacity for life don't need more than the basics. How can they? They have no capacity. Whereas he — he had tremendous capacity for life. So he satisfied his larger desires. It was simple.

Along with his fetish for fine timepieces, Woolsey had a second religion: golf. A scratch golfer, he purchased memberships at two golf clubs where the beautiful people played — Winged Foot Golf Club in Westchester and Beacon Hill Golf Club in New Jersey. He took two vacations, one to Florida and one to Vermont, and he golfed every day during both. There were some beautiful courses in Florida. Most of them had nearby five-star restaurants. So after a day on the links, Monsignor Woolsey dropped $500 on dinner and wine. It was very relaxing. And he needed to relax what with all his responsibilities.

In 1999, a month after Easter, Monsignor Woolsey lunched again with Rose Cale. They talked. They were old friends now and could say anything to one another. As usual, talk turned to money and investments.

"I recently purchased a block of high-tech stocks," said Monsignor Woolsey. He reached for his glass of wine — a very fine 1995 Rombauer Chardonnay.

"I wish I had the courage to jump into those," said Rose. "But my broker always cautions me about them. He says they're risky."

Monsignor Woolsey nodded. "Big risk means a big pay

day." He smiled. "Or a big loss. Your broker is correct to warn you."

"Yes, I guess so," Rose said. "But still . . . it seems like a small investment wouldn't hurt."

"You're a very perceptive woman, Rose," said the monsignor, showing a dazzling smile. Perfect teeth that were perfectly white stood out against his deep tan. "That's why I enjoy your company so much," he added.

Rose blushed. She loved being seen in public with him. He was so handsome and so famous. "Thank you, John," she said. She stabbed her fork into her salad. "I just wish my broker were a little more flexible. I mean, it is my money."

Woolsey shrugged. "Perhaps you should make a change," he suggested.

"What do you mean, John?"

"Simply this. If you want more diversification in your financial portfolio, perhaps it's time to diversify your investments." He took a sip of wine.

"Hmmm," said Rose. "Maybe you're right." She leaned closer. "It's just that I don't want to hurt anyone's feelings."

"That's because you're a kind person," said the monsignor, reaching across the table to press her hand. "But this isn't about feelings, Rose. This is business. Something altogether different."

Rose nodded. "You're right, of course."

Woolsey chuckled. "Let's change the subject. The last thing I want to do is pressure you or tell you what to do with your money." He picked up his glass of wine and swirled the pale yellow liquid around. "If God blesses my investments, do you know what I want to do with it? What my hopes and plans are?"

"What?" asked Rose, dabbing her mouth with her napkin.

Monsignor Woolsey stared out the window of the restaurant. "There's a small condominium in New Jersey. It's on the beach. You can hear the waves crashing while you lie in bed." He looked at Rose. "That's what I hope to do. Buy myself a small condo on the beach in New Jersey. A place where I can get away from it all." He looked at her, gauging her response.

"What a wonderful dream, John," Rose said. "I didn't know you were such a homebody. You're always on the go all the time."

"That's because I didn't think I'd ever be able to afford my dream, Rose. Priests don't usually have the luxury of owning a home. Like me, they live in the city rectory."

Rose smiled and held out her hand. He leaned forward and took it. A wonderful idea popped into her head.

"John," said Rose, "I want to make your dream a reality. One that does not depend on the rise and fall of the stock market."

Woolsey gave her a calculatedly puzzled look. "What do you mean, dear Rose?"

Rose sat up straight and smiled. "I want to buy the condo for you," she said.

"No, no, no," said the monsignor, shaking his head and leaning back in his chair. "I didn't mean to suggest that — I was just telling you what I was thinking."

"And I'm just telling you what I'm thinking," said Rose. "I want to do this. You're my friend, and I insist that you let me buy you a condo."

"I don't know, Rose," said the monsignor, injecting doubt into his tone.

"It's settled," said Rose. "I won't take no for an answer. Besides, it's the least you can let me do."

"You're quite a woman, Rose. Quite a woman." He leaned forward and took both of her hands in his. "Thank you. Thank you very much."

Rose blushed once again. "Now," she said. "There's something I want you to do for me."

"Anything," said Monsignor Woolsey.

"I want you to transfer my account with Prudential Securities into an account with your broker," she said. "That way I can avoid hurting anyone, and —" she smiled at him — "I make a smart business decision at the same time."

Smiling back at her, Woolsey shook his head playfully. "You're a regular dynamo today, aren't you? My goodness. I am impressed." He paused. "You know, of course, since it's a new account, it would probably have to be opened in both our names."

Rose waved a hand at him, as if she was brushing something out of the air. "I don't care about the details, John. I just want to know that you'll do this for me?"

He laughed. "Of course, dear Rose," he said. "What are friends for?"

Two days later Rose Cale gave Monsignor John Woolsey $100,000. He immediately called his real estate agent and bought a condominium at the Channel Club Tower in Monmouth Beach, New Jersey. The condo had two bedrooms and two bathrooms and boasted luxurious appointments: hardwood floors, real tile flooring in the kitchen, top-of-the-line appliances, and a hot tub on the back deck.

On the same day, Rose's stock portfolio was transferred from Prudential Securities. A new account was opened with Woolsey's broker. The names on the new account were John Woolsey and Rose Cale. The portfolio was worth $400,000.

Three months later, in August, Woolsey boarded a flight for Spain, where he spent the next two weeks playing golf on the beautiful and challenging Spanish courses.

Before he left for the airport, he had dinner with Rose at the Lenox Room, one of Manhattan's finest restaurants. He had broiled swordfish, sugared baby potatoes, and crème brulé for dessert. Rose had the same, except she selected cherries jubilee for dessert. Two bottles of 1992 Opus One accompanied the meal. As they left the Lenox Room, Rose slipped a white envelope to Monsignor Woolsey.

Once he was comfortably settled in his first-class seat on the airplane, he opened the envelope. It held $5,000 in cash. Fifty $100 bills. There was also a handwritten note: "A little spending money." It was signed "Your loving friend, Rose." Woolsey opened his mouth in a silent laugh. Then he crumpled the note and the envelope and shoved them into the seat pocket.

Turning to the blonde stewardess, he said, "Do you have any champagne?"

"Certainly, Father," she said.

Dressed in his black cassock with red piping, he looked elegant. The stewardess thought he looked like Kirk Douglas.

One year later, in May 2000, Monsignor Woolsey pulled into the valet parking at Petaluma, a concept restaurant in Manhattan. Petaluma catered to image-conscious yuppies, the kind of people who worried about how they looked and wanted a pleasing setting against which to pose.

Petaluma served delicious food. Not only did it taste good, but the presentation of the food also delighted the self-absorbed expectations of the people who were paying for it. Beautiful food for beautiful people.

Handing the keys to his tan Lexus to the valet, Monsignor

Woolsey walked into the restaurant. As he entered, people turned and stared. It wasn't every day you saw Kirk Douglas in Manhattan wearing a black cassock trimmed with red.

Woolsey smiled graciously as the hostess led him to his usual table. In keeping with the image-concept of Petaluma, the hostess wore a violet silk suit. Walking behind her, Woolsey gave his silent, open-mouthed laugh. He loved this place.

Rose Cale sat waiting for him at the table. Dressed in spring pink, she looked pale and very old. Especially when compared to the vibrant, hip, successful yuppies around her.

"My dear Rose," said Monsignor Woolsey, taking her hand and kissing her cheek. "How are you?"

"John," said Rose, "seeing you always perks me up."

"Well, that's good," said the monsignor, "but it leads me to conclude that you're not feeling well. Healthwise, I mean."

"I'm getting old, John," said Rose, a serious note in her voice.

Woolsey shook his head in protest. "You are not," he said. "It's just been a long winter. Now that it's spring you'll feel better. Just wait and see."

A waiter approached, and they ordered.

"John," said Rose, "I want to ask you something."

"Of course," replied the monsignor. "What's up?"

"It's about my will," she said. Then she held up a hand to stop his objection. "Let me finish, please. As you know, my brother Frank is the beneficiary of my estate. When I die, I was wondering if you would mind being a sort of, well, an unofficial executor of the will?"

"I don't understand, my dear Rose," said Woolsey. "Isn't your accountant the executor?"

"Yes."

"Then why on Earth would you need me to check up on

him? Because, really, that's what I'd be doing."

"I know," Rose said, nodding. "I just want to be sure that Frank is taken care of. Properly, you know? He's so frail and nearly deaf. And all he has right now is his monthly pittance from Social Security." She paused, then said, "And I worry about him."

Monsignor Woolsey smiled. "I know you do. And that's because you are one of life's rarities — a person with a good and pure heart."

Rose blushed.

"But really, Rose, your will states what you desire. Your accountant has to see that it is carried out according to what it says. There's nothing to worry about."

"I know," said Rose. "But I can't stop worrying. He's my only living relative. He's all the family I have."

"You've got me, too, don't forget," said the monsignor, smiling. "And if it eases your mind, I'll do whatever you ask."

Their drinks arrived. A glass of Chardonnay for Woolsey and a vodka and tonic for Rose.

Woolsey took a sip and tapped the glass lightly. "That's good. How's yours?"

"Very nice," said Rose.

"You know, Rose, I was just thinking. Poor Frank, with all his disabilities, might have a difficult time. I mean there's bills to be paid, checks to write, maintenance on the house, grocery shopping, cleaning — a million things to do and keep track of." He took another sip of wine. "Do you think Frank can do all that?"

Rose shook her head. "No, I don't. And that worries me too."

"Of course, I'll be there," said the monsignor, "to help in any manner I can. Yet — well, never mind."

"Yet what?" prompted Rose.

"Well, I was just going to say that it might be easier for Frank, and for me too, if I were to have more control," said Woolsey.

"How do you mean?" said Rose, signaling for another vodka and tonic.

The monsignor held up his hand. "Now this is just a suggestion," he said. "But since we're agreed that Frank will find it difficult — indeed almost impossible — to take care of himself, and since the executor — your accountant — won't have time to do what needs to be done, well, I just thought it might be more advantageous if I were able to do whatever needed to be done. For Frank."

"You're right, of course, John," said Rose. "But how can I be sure that Frank is taken care of?"

Monsignor Woolsey finished his wine with a gulp. "The only way you can be absolutely certain of Frank's welfare," he said, "is to name someone else as the beneficiary of your will. Someone that you know and trust. Someone that will watch over Frank like family."

He picked up his menu and began to scan it while Rose sat thinking. "I think," said the monsignor, "that a BLT sounds awfully good. I haven't had one in ages. And between you and me, I'm getting a little tired of all this other stuff." He tossed his menu on the table and looked at Rose. "What are you having?"

"John," said Rose. Her face glowed with excitement. "I just had the most wonderful idea. Almost like God himself dropped the idea right into my head."

Monsignor Woolsey made a questioning gesture with his hands.

"You," said Rose. "I'm going to name you as my beneficiary. That way I'll be sure that Frank is in good hands."

A smile slowly spread across Woolsey's face. "You know, Rose," he said casually, "that just might work."

"Of course it will work," asserted Rose. "You said it yourself. Someone who is family. Who else but you?" She smiled at him. "I don't know why I didn't think of it sooner."

Monsignor Woolsey shrugged and raised his eyebrows. "You're right! Wisdom from heaven. It is the only way we can assure Frank's welfare."

Rose pursed her lips, exhaling happily. "What a relief!" she said. "Now I can sleep at night knowing my dearest Frank is in the hands of family." She waved the waiter over. "I'll have another vodka and tonic. And another glass of wine for my friend — the monsignor."

The monsignor leaned back in his chair and smiled.

"I'll change my will immediately," announced Rose.

"Could you wait until after we eat?" said the monsignor, chuckling.

Rose gave him a wide-eyed stare, then laughed.

The very next day Rose Cale instructed her attorney to draw up a new will, naming Monsignor John Woolsey as sole beneficiary. Her house and all its furnishings would go to Woolsey when she died. Her stocks and jewelry and cash — valued at $1.3 million — would also go to the monsignor.

With the revised will in an envelope, Rose had her chauffeur drive her to St. John the Martyr Catholic Church. There, in the presence of Monsignor Woolsey and members of his office staff, she signed the document with a flourish. Woolsey hugged her.

Then they all had cookies and coffee.

Rose Cale's accountant was Janet Naegele. Smart, pretty, and painfully honest, Naegele was shocked when Rose told her the will was to be changed. Rose had never married or had any children. As far as Janet knew, Rose had never even had a boyfriend.

Rose had three siblings: her brother Frank and two sisters, both of whom had passed away years ago. None of the four Cales had ever married or had children. They were a very tight-knit group, affectionate only to each other. To the Cales, family was literally everything.

Which was why Janet was shocked. Frank was all the family Rose had left. She would never abandon him or cut him out of her will. It was unimaginable. So what was going on?

Janet found out what was going on soon enough. Rose told her the name of the new beneficiary. Janet didn't know Monsignor John Woolsey personally, but she had read about him in the *New York Times*. He was very involved in religious crusades of one type or another — very popular and undeniably photogenic. Janet decided that either Rose had finally gone bonkers like other old women she'd read about who left all their money to television preachers or there had been undue influence. Which meant that someone was manipulating this gullible old lady to get her money.

At the moment, Janet couldn't do much other than ask Rose if she was sure this was what she wanted. Janet could not tell her she was wrong. Not yet anyway. But Janet could and would do some investigating. Monsignor Woolsey had some explaining to do.

Three months later Janet arrived at St. John the Martyr Catholic Church. She parked her car and marched into the old and ornate church. A hush of piety hung in the air as if angels had been singing but stopped when someone walked in. She found the church offices, which sat off to the side, near the back. Janet asked a young secretary if Monsignor Woolsey was available.

"Sure," said the secretary. She motioned for Janet to follow her. Then she walked to an open door and stuck her head in. "John," she said. "Someone to see you."

A finely tuned baritone voice replied, and the secretary waved Janet in.

Janet took a deep breath and walked through the doorway, mentally whispering to herself, "Childe Roland to the dark tower came," which was from Robert Browning's poem of the same name.

There he was. Tall and tanned and handsome. A warm smile showed off his perfect teeth. He wore a black cassock with red trim. He reminded Janet of someone. Some movie star.

"Welcome," boomed the monsignor. "I'm Monsignor Woolsey. But everyone around here calls me John. Have a seat, please," he said, gesturing at a chair.

"No, thank you," said Janet in a frosty voice.

On the drive over, she had decided not to sit. And definitely not to engage in any small talk. She had to come right to the point, say what she had to say. If not, she was certain that, like the serpent in the Garden of Eden, he would charm her. Then she'd be lost.

Just for an instant, Monsignor Woolsey hesitated. But he recovered well. And his dazzling smile didn't fade even a bit. "What can we — the church and I — do for you?" he said, radiating bewitching curiosity.

"I'm the executrix of Rose Cale's estate," announced Janet. "And I'm here to inform you that I'm going to challenge Ms. Cale's will as it now stands."

The smile drooped from his face. Then it was back, only now it looked stiff. "Why would you do that?" the monsignor said. His blue eyes looked icy.

"Because I believe," said Janet, "that undue influence has occurred. That Ms. Cale's will does not reflect her true wishes."

"Is that so?"

"Yes. I also think it only fair to warn you that I will be lodging a complaint to the Archdiocese of New York this very afternoon," said Janet. Her voice quivered with stress.

"Since you brought it up," said the monsignor, "may I inquire what you are complaining about? To the archdiocese?"

"That you wheedled almost half a million dollars from Ms. Cale. And that you then induced her to change her will, naming you as the beneficiary," said Janet.

Monsignor Woolsey chuckled. "There seems to be some misunderstanding," he said. "Rose has been very generous to St. John the Martyr." He made a sweeping motion with his hand to include the building. "She has also been very generous to me. She gave me $80,000 once, I believe. As for the will —"

Janet cut him off. "The will reflects persuasion of the most pernicious type," said Janet, almost hissing.

Monsignor Woolsey stood staring at her. His smile was gone.

"That's all I have to say," said Janet, turning toward the door.

After the woman left, Woolsey remained standing. Pursing his lips, he thought about what had just happened. He realized he didn't even know the woman's name.

Sixty seconds later he sat down behind his desk. Reaching

for his cell phone, he speed-dialed a number.

In the offices of attorney Christopher Houlihan, the phone rang.

Janet Naegele drove to the Archdiocese of New York. She was still shaking inside from her confrontation with Monsignor Woolsey. By the time she arrived, she had calmed down, but every once in a while her right hand trembled.

Inside the building that housed the offices of the Archdiocese of New York of the American Roman Catholic Church, Janet was ushered into the presence of a middle-aged man dressed in a business suit. She had expected a priest.

The man introduced himself as a diocesan attorney. If she had a complaint, he would listen to it. Then, after due consideration, he would determine if the complaint urged further investigation.

Janet accepted a cup of coffee, then told him a story about an old woman and her will and a monsignor.

One week after her meeting at the archdiocese, Janet received a phone call. It was the diocesan attorney. In a short, clipped tone, he told her that, based upon her complaint, the archdiocese had begun an investigation. If anything came to light, she would be advised. The man cautioned her that sensitive investigations of this type usually took some time to complete. So she should not be concerned if she didn't hear anything immediately. Janet thanked the man for his call.

Rose Cale's health was going from bad to worse, and Janet was trying to get Rose to change her will again.

"You must void this will," said Janet, shaking the document, "and write a new one. Frank should be named as the beneficiary, and I will be the executrix."

"I don't know," said Rose. She felt as if she was being attacked. "The monsignor —"

Janet jumped in. "The monsignor is a wolf in sheep's clothing. And this document stinks," said Janet.

Finally, after weeks of nagging and cajoling by Janet and many other people, Rose decided she had made a mistake. She changed her will. Frank would get the house and the stocks and the money. Janet Naegele, the Cale family's long-time friend and accountant, would be the executrix.

One month later, 2003, Rose Cale passed away. Her funeral mass was performed by a Roman Catholic priest. It was not Monsignor John Woolsey.

Frank Cale, thin, weak, and almost stone deaf, asserted himself. "I won't allow it. I won't have that phoney-baloney priest — Woolsey — at her funeral," he said in a watery voice.

Meanwhile, the archdiocese's investigation proceeded. Strange irregularities materialized like ghost sightings in the financial books of St. John the Martyr. And Monsignor Woolsey's personal extravagances seemed suspicious. In short, Woolsey had an awful lot of money, went on awfully nice vacations, and ate in awfully expensive restaurants for someone who made $15,000 a year. Something awful was up.

Janet Naegele got tired of waiting. Upset by Rose's death, and by how close Frank had come to losing everything, Janet decided to take action. This kind of criminal behavior could not go on. Someone had to take responsibility to stop it. Janet would. Someone was accountable — Monsignor Woolsey. Janet hired an attorney.

On Monday, July 12, 2004, Janet Naegele's attorney filed

suit, and the next day all hell broke loose. The *New York Daily News* reported that a lawsuit had been filed against Monsignor John Woolsey and the Archdiocese of New York.

"As a Catholic, I am outraged by the conduct at issue in this case," Janet told the *Daily News*. "Priests and pastors, who are revered by their parishioners, should not accept large personal gifts from them."

Naegele's suit claimed that Monsignor Woolsey had swindled Rose Cale, "a devout elderly parishioner," out of $500,000. The monsignor, insisted the suit, used the money to buy himself a condo. Then, after bilking the meek woman out of $490,000 in cash and stocks, he convinced her to name him the sole beneficiary of her estate. Woolsey did this by "exercising undue influence on Miss Cale and was able to manipulate her to his personal gain. These representations of material facts by Monsignor Woolsey were false, known by Monsignor Woolsey to be false. Over time, Monsignor Woolsey interjected himself into Miss Cale's daily affairs of both a personal and business nature." The lawsuit also insisted that the cardinal of New York, Edward Egan, was to blame for Monsignor Woolsey's "reprehensible conduct."

It was as if a bomb from hell had just exploded in heaven.

Archdiocesan spokesman Joseph Zwilling said, "We haven't seen the lawsuit yet, so I can't respond to that." When asked about Monsignor Woolsey, Zwilling spoke cautiously while at the same time trying to distance the archdiocese from the monsignor. His only comment was "That's between the estate and him." Zwilling went on to add that the Archdiocese of New York had been conducting its own investigation into the matter. Upon learning of the lawsuit, the archdiocese had immediately turned over all its findings to the office of the Manhattan District Attorney.

Zwilling didn't say so, but that act of turning over the find-ings insinuated that the archdiocese thought Monsignor Woolsey was a renegade priest and guilty as hell.

Woolsey's attorney was unavailable, which wasn't unusual. Defense attorneys usually speak only when it is in their client's best interests.

The answering machine at St. John the Martyr told callers that, "due to a technical media overload," calls were not being accepted. In other words, everyone had been told to keep his or her mouth shut.

Members of St. John the Martyr Church were bewildered by the accusations. "He's a very good person," said Laura Aponte. "He wants to help people. I don't think he would take advantage of anyone."

Like Roman lions, the media pounced on other priests, questioning them about Monsignor Woolsey's character and about donations in their churches. Father Michael Green said, "I know nothing of the charges. I don't want to hear." The pastor of St. Ignatius Loyola Church, Father Walter Modrys, said many parishioners had attempted to give him gifts. He relayed the story of once giving the sacrament of the sick to one of his members. "She looked up and said, 'You know, Father, I'm giving my money to the church.' I said, 'If this sacrament works the way it's supposed to, that's a long way off.'" The woman died later and left several hundred thousand dollars to St. Ignatius. "There was no possibility of undue influence," said the priest.

One priest from the Bronx agreed to speak only if his name was not used. He stated that he had taken one of his members to the hospital. Then he found $20,000 in her house. He told the woman about the money and asked her what she wanted him to do with it. The woman told him to take it. He refused. Later he used the money to pay for her nursing home and, when she died, her funeral expenses. He gave the rest to a charity. "What was I supposed to do?" he asked. "I had to take care of her."

A reporter asked frail, almost deaf, Frank Cale what he thought of the Church. "They're a bunch of lousy . . . ," said Frank, stopping himself just in time. "I am very disappointed in the church."

Three days later, on July 16, 2004, the Archdiocese of New York took steps. Given the media flurry, the Church couldn't afford to look wishy-washy. It ordered Monsignor John Woolsey to resign as pastor of St. John the Martyr Church. Zwilling, the spokesman, said that the archdiocese was taking this action because of the misuse of parish monies, not because of the lawsuit.

The order to resign was delivered to Woolsey by Father Desmond O'Connor, the director of priest personnel. He and Woolsey were close friends. Father O'Connor did not want to do it, but he had to. The princes of the Church had decided.

At the same time that Zwilling was making his statement, Monsignor Woolsey came out of the sacristy at St. John the Martyr Church. Dressed in his black cassock with the crimson trim of his office, he walked to the front of the altar. The people began to applaud. Holding up his hands for silence, the monsignor spoke to the faithful who had gathered in the sanctuary.

"There is absolutely no truth to the charge of undue influence on Ms. Cale," he said. "If I ever tried to tell her what to do with her money, she would have told me what to do."

The congregation chuckled.

"The notion that she was someone who could be easily manipulated is an insult to her memory," said Monsignor Woolsey. "Rose Cale was a generous person. She gave freely to this church. Every nickel that she gave went to benefit the church."

That was all he had to say. He disappeared back into the sacristy.

Afterward, William Donohue, president of the Catholic League for Religious and Civil Rights, said Monsignor Woolsey was not guilty of anything except lax bookkeeping. Standing outside the church, Donohue told reporters, "He'd be the first one to say that when it comes to my bookkeeping measures, there's a lot to be desired. But they've been going through his records, and he's been able to demonstrate most, if not all, of where this went, where that went. There's a difference between sloppy bookkeeping and some kind of criminal who has made an attempt to fleece the archdiocese or shake down some old lady." Donohue hastened to add, "I have known Monsignor Woolsey as a friend for over a decade and consider him to be one of the finest priests I have ever met. That is why I am so disturbed to learn that he is being tried in the court of public opinion over charges that have a strange odor to them. He deserves better than this."

Donohue had been president of the Catholic League since 1993. It was not part of the Roman Catholic Church. It was a private organization that sought to promote and defend Catholics and their beliefs. It was a powerful group.

Donohue himself had been described as pragmatic and media savvy by some people. Others, especially women, used stronger language. They characterized him as abusive and a total media hound. Laughing at these criticisms, Donohue bluntly stated that his confrontational style got immediate results. He didn't have time for unproductive nonsense.

A powerful ally, Donohue took up Monsignor Woolsey's fight as his own because the monsignor, like Donohue, was a diehard when it came to Catholic doctrine. At a press conference, he said, "It has been alleged that Monsignor Woolsey would often dine with Rose Cale, the elderly woman who generously gave to his parish. Now how about that? Isn't that proof positive he's a hustler? Even worse, he is alleged to have escorted her to her doctor's office! Is this the kind of behavior we expect from priests? How sly of him to do so! And to top it off, there is evidence that Monsignor Woolsey actually signed letters to her, 'Love, Msgr. Woolsey.'" Sneering, Donohue then said, "The kicker is this — lawyers have evidently concluded that he did not sign all of his letters this way. They're so right: having personally received letters of thanks from Msgr. Woolsey for occasionally taking him to dinner, never once did he sign off, "Love, Msgr. Woolsey.' Enter this as Exhibit A."

In the end, Donohue failed as the devil's advocate.

Monsignor Woolsey resigned from his pastorate at St. John the Martyr Church. He did it quietly. There was no press conference.

The investigation by the Manhattan District Attorney's office proceeded. All records from St. John the Martyr were seized, along with all the computers. Woolsey's bank accounts were first frozen, then seized.

One year later — almost to the day — Manhattan District Attorney Robert M. Morgenthau announced the indictment of sixty-seven-year-old Monsignor John Woolsey. The charges were grand larceny, tax evasion, and falsifying business records for the purpose of embezzlement. Investigators determined that Woolsey had plundered $836,744.58 from the parish by funneling $820,000 from parish accounts into his personal bank accounts. He had also used money from the parish checking account to pay off his personal credit card to the tune of $15,944.58.

Investigators discovered that Woolsey had spent $200,000 of the stolen money on Rolex, Breitling, Omega, and Breguet watches. He had bought clothing for himself from Macy's and Bloomingdale's. Other large amounts of stolen money had been spent on meals and wine at Petaluma and Lenox Room. Woolsey had purchased top-of-the-line golf equipment and paid for country club expenses and travel expenses to Vermont, Florida, and Spain.

The same afternoon Monsignor Woolsey surrendered to police detectives from the NYPD District Attorney's Office Squad. The two detectives escorted Woolsey to jail, where he was booked, his photo was taken, and he was fingerprinted.

Because he was a priest, he wasn't issued jail clothing. He was allowed to wear his black cassock with the red trim. And, thankfully, he was not strip-searched. The correction officers were Catholics and thought it might be a sin to humiliate a priest.

Two hours later Woolsey was arraigned in New York State Supreme Court, Room 70. Standing next to his attorney, Woolsey listened as the court clerk read the charges. With each sentence spoken, he grew more pale despite his golf course tan. Grand Larceny in the Second Degree, a C felony punishable by up to fifteen years in prison; Grand Larceny in the Third Degree, a D felony punishable by up to seven years in prison; four counts of Filing a False Personal Tax Return with Intent to Evade Tax; four counts of Offering a False Instrument for Filing in the First Degree; and six counts of Falsifying Business Records in the First Degree, all E felonies punishable by up to four years in prison. All together, Monsignor Woolsey was charged with sixteen felonies. He was looking at seventy-eight years in prison if they threw the book at him.

"How do you plead?" asked Supreme Court Justice Michael Ambrecht.

Monsignor Woolsey whispered to his attorney. The attorney, whose name was Nicholas DeFeis, said something only his client could hear.

Seated in the room were a dozen or more members of St. John the Martyr Church. They had come in support of their pastor. As they waited for him to speak, they held their breath.

Looking at the judge, Monsignor Woolsey said, "Not guilty."

Prosecutor Matthew Amatruda said, "Your Honor, the people request no bail and that the defendant be held in jail during the course of these proceedings."

"Why is that?" asked the judge.

"The people perceive a definite flight risk, Your Honor," said Amatruda.

DeFeis scoffed. "Your Honor, there is no risk of flight. My client surrendered himself of his own free will."

"I agree with the defense," said the judge. "I see no risk of flight."

The prosecutor's face tightened. "But Your Honor, the charges imply deceit and a great deal of cleverness. The people request no bail because of the imminent risk of flight."

Justice Ambrecht thought for a moment. Looking at Monsignor Woolsey, he said, "Monsignor, I am releasing you on your own recognizance. You will, however, surrender your passport to the court."

Woolsey left the courtroom with his attorney. Outside the courtroom, a throng of reporters and television cameras crushed forward, surrounding the two men. Nicholas DeFeis stopped and said to Woolsey, "Let me do the talking."

"I will make a brief statement," said DeFeis, addressing the throng of reporters. "The only money he," said DeFeis, nodding his head at Monsignor Woolsey, "ever spent on himself came from contributions that parishioners permitted him to use personally because he was doing a great job as their pastor and shouldn't have to get by on the meager $15,000 a year that he received as compensation from the archdiocese." Then DeFeis pointed to the many supporters who had followed them out of the courtroom. "There is obviously another side to this story. My client is innocent of all the charges, and we will prove it in there." He darted a finger at the courtroom. DeFeis grinned. "He may not have been a good bookkeeper, but he was a beloved, effective, and honest pastor."

Reporters shouted out questions. DeFeis shook his head and pressed through the wall of bodies and cameras. Woolsey followed in his wake.

Excited and afraid at the same time, the monsignor didn't know whether he was 98% excited and 2% afraid or 2% excited and 98% afraid. He liked the media's attention even under these circumstances because he didn't believe there was such a thing as negative publicity. All publicity was good in Monsignor Woolsey's opinion. Being the center of attention thrilled Woolsey.

What scared him was that no one seemed to understand. He wasn't a bad person. He had devoted the past forty years of his life to others. And now this. He wanted to scream out at them, "You don't understand!" He offered this defense to a reporter who interviewed him.

Eight months later, on March 8, 2006, New York State Supreme Court Justice Bruce Allen made a decision.

Woolsey's attorneys had filed a motion to have the charges against the monsignor dismissed. The attorneys argued that the prosecutors had conducted their grand jury proceedings improperly and that the evidence against the monsignor was insufficient to bring him to trial.

According to the defense attorneys, the prosecutors had screwed up. When they presented their evidence to the grand jury, the prosecutors did not call in an expert on canon law. This expert — if he had been present — would have told the grand jury that Woolsey might have thought he had a "claim of right" to the money. In other words, as the pastor and treasurer of the church, and as the co-vicar (deputy bishop) of East Manhattan, he could claim the money was his by title and authority. Under church rules, that is. The point the defense attorneys were trying to make was this: if the money was already his by claim of right, then it wasn't stolen. There was no case because there was no crime. Therefore, dismissal was the only reasonable course. To support their argument, the defense attorneys also gave the judge affidavits from parishioners who declared they donated money to the church and did not care whether, in fact expected, Monsignor Woolsey to use part of it for personal expenses.

In other words, everybody — except the grand jury — understood what was going on. And the grand jury would have understood if the expert had been present. The expert in canon law could have told the grand jury that it was not stealing if everybody, even the parishioners, knew and believed Monsignor Woolsey had a "claim of right."

Justice Allen wasn't buying it. "For me to allow that," he said with a skeptical look on his face, "there would have to be evidence that Monsignor Woolsey had a good faith belief that he was entitled to the money." Peering over the rims of his glasses, Justice Allen added, "And there ain't no such evidence. Is there?"

The defense attorneys didn't move a muscle.

"Therefore," continued Justice Allen, taking their silence as agreement, "the expert's testimony was, as the prosecutors contend, an irrelevant abstraction. The prosecutors were not obligated to call him as a witness or to inform the grand jurors of his availability."

Justice Allen glanced through his notes. Then he said, "As to the other matter, the unspoken expectations of a donor would not transform a donation to a church into a personal gift to its pastor. As I do not find that the grand jury proceedings were defective, the motion to dismiss is denied."

The defense attorneys looked at each other and shrugged. It had been worth a try. Now it was time for a plea bargain.

DeFeis didn't pull any punches when he put it to Monsignor Woolsey. "Look, John," the lawyer said to the now-sixty-eight-year-old priest. "Either you plead guilty to a lesser charge, or you're going to spend your golden years in prison. When you get out, you'll be eighty-three years old."

A drying realization spread through Monsignor Woolsey, as if someone was preheating an oven. He felt sick to his soul.

"Hell," snorted DeFeis, "it's a no-brainer. We'll cut the deal."

So the defense attorneys began negotiations for a plea bargain. The prosecutors were reluctant to cut a deal. But in the end, they did because they didn't want to put Woolsey on the witness stand. They realized that, once he got up there with his clergy collar and his black cassock and his charming smile and his debonair manner, . . . well, the jury was going to believe him. And they — the prosecutors — would look like silly liars. Then the defense attorneys would toss out words such as *religious persecution* and *witch hunt*. The media would pick up on it, and a bad dream would become the ultimate nightmare from hell.

The prosecution had a good case and would probably win. If they did win, Monsignor Woolsey would go to prison for fifteen years. But the prosecutors asked themselves, "Is it worth it?" Shit happens, as the saying goes, and the whole thing might blow up in their faces. Anytime anyone put a priest on a witness stand there was no way of predicting what a jury might do.

It was a no-win situation. If the prosecutors cut Monsignor Woolsey a deal, at least they could put him away for a little while. They would look good. Justice would be served.

On May 27, 2006, court was in session. The people versus Monsignor John Woolsey.

Prosecutor Matthew Amatruda addressed Justice Bruce Allen. "Your Honor, Monsignor Woolsey spent $250,000 on expensive watches, like Rolexes and Breitlings. And on golf outings, trips to Europe, designer clothes, and cosmetic dentistry."

Justice Allen hadn't heard the part about the cosmetic dentistry before. He glanced over at the priest. So that was why the monsignor's smile looked like an advertisement on a billboard for a Hollywood dentist.

Amatruda continued reciting the priest's crimes. "Monsignor Woolsey hid the stolen money in a secret bank account, falsified church records to conceal his thefts, and then lied to his superiors in the archdiocese about where the money had gone." The prosecutor paused to take a breath. "Your Honor," Amatruda intoned, "he was quite literally cashing in on his role as administrator and spiritual leader of his parish. Monsignor Woolsey used greed, manipulation, and opportunism to abuse the position of trust he had been given."

The prosecutor was ready to conclude. He had been building up to make his final point.

"Our recommendation to the court is for two to six years in prison. And restitution in the amount of $830,000," he said.

"Thank you," said Justice Allen. He already knew what was going to happen. All parties had agreed to the plea bargain. This was just a formality. He looked at Nicholas DeFeis. "Your turn, counselor," said the judge.

"Thank you, Your Honor," said DeFeis. "My client, Monsignor Woolsey, suffers from a psychological condition. His condition should be considered a mitigating factor in his sentencing, Your Honor."

Justice Allen didn't say anything.

"Monsignor Woolsey would like to read a statement at this time, Your Honor," said DeFeis. "He has changed his plea from not guilty to guilty in one count of second-degree grand larceny."

Very fit and tanned, Woolsey stood up. His black cassock with red trim was immaculate. With his silver hair brushed back from his forehead, he looked like an older version of Richard Chamberlain in *The Thorn Birds*. He began reading from a paper he held in his perfectly manicured hands. "I admit that I stole at least $50,000 from the Church of St. John the Martyr, while serving as the pastor of the church. However, Your Honor, it was my belief that since the people of my parish were so devoted to me that I had their permission and discretion to use church money for my personal needs." Woolsey hoped the "claim of right" idea might buy him some leniency. That's why he brought it up. "I recognize that the amount I spent on myself exceeded any lawful entitlement. I am deeply sorry for my actions, and I apologize for my conduct." Woolsey gave the court a dazzling smile and sat down.

Justice Allen was not charmed. "Monsignor," he said, "I can tell you this. Your sentence will encompass one to five years in prison. I will, however, consider a lesser sentence if I am satisfied with the amount of money you agree to pay by way of restitution."

DeFeis jumped in. "Your Honor, Monsignor Woolsey has already paid $200,000 in restitution."

Justice Allen nodded his understanding. "Sentencing will take place September 22."

Nick DeFeis and Monsignor Woolsey dined at the Lenox Room that evening. They were celebrating a half-victory. Sentencing had yet to take place, but it couldn't be worse than five years in prison. Which was a hell of a lot better than fifteen years. And DeFeis was confident that the court would lean toward the low end — probably one year.

"Heck," said DeFeis, buttering his roll, "there's a strong probability you could get off with only community service."

"You think so?" asked Monsignor Woolsey.

"Yes," said DeFeis. "I do. And let me tell you why." He leaned across the table and pointed at the monsignor's clergy collar. "Because of that," he said. Then he took a bite of his roll, talking as he chewed. "No one wants to throw a Roman Catholic priest into prison. It doesn't look good. So if I were the judge, I'd lecture you a little bit in a stern voice. Then I'd

RANDALL RADIC

slap your hands and sentence you to a thousand hours of community service. With a stiff fine, reminding you to make restitution."

"You think that's what he'll do?" said Monsignor Woolsey. He didn't have much appetite. So he focused on the two bottles of wine at their table. He was still worried. Not as worried as he had been, but just the same he didn't want to spend time in prison. Even if it was a minimum-security prison. Anger bubbled through him too. Anger at the prosecutor's insinuation that he had betrayed a sacred trust. He had done no such thing, he told his attorney. The money had been given to him to use as he saw fit. After all, he was Monsignor Woolsey, co-vicar of East Manhattan — almost a bishop.

"I can almost guarantee it," said DeFeis. "It's the expedient thing to do under the circumstances." He reached for another roll. "You sure you don't want one? They're delicious."

Woolsey reached for his glass of wine. "No thanks," he said, thinking about what DeFeis had just said. It made sense. He could relax. It would all work out. Smiling at DeFeis, the monsignor poured himself another glass of wine.

It was September 22, 2006. The courtroom was packed. Journalists, friends, fans, and enemies — they were all there to witness the sentencing of Father Flim Flam, the nickname the newspapers had given to Monsignor John Woolsey. Everyone gawked and whispered. The buzzing whispers sounded like a leaking steam pipe. Everyone had an opinion. And everyone wanted to be sure that everyone else heard that opinion. Even the bailiffs looked interested.

Woolsey sat next to his attorney at the table reserved for the defense. If he looked to the right, he saw a similar table, where the three prosecutors and their assistants sat.

Justice Bruce Allen entered unannounced and sat down. He looked at one of the bailiffs and nodded.

The bailiff stepped forward and said, "Quiet in the court, please."

"Before I sentence you, do you have anything to say?" Justice Allen asked Monsignor Woolsey.

The monsignor rose to his feet. His black cassock with red trim draped almost to his ankles.

"First I would like to again apologize," said Woolsey. "God willing, I would turn back the clock. Which I can't do. I have felt the sting of comments when I was down. As a result of my sufferings, I will be more conscious of someone who is down — more sympathetic and less judgmental.

"Like Moses, when God told him to hold up his arms until the battle was won, I, too, have felt my arms grown tired. When I could hold them up no longer, my followers came along and held up each of my arms. Just like Moses.

"I am grateful to my supporters for sticking by me."

Woolsey turned and gave the onlookers a dazzling smile. Then the monsignor sat down.

"You should know that across the street in Criminal Court, people who steal cans of tuna fish wind up going to jail for thirty days or fifty days," said Justice Allen. "Your crime concerns much more than that. Much more — almost $1 million."

He stood up and leaned over his bench, looking straight into Monsignor Woolsey's blue eyes. The judge smiled. "I seriously considered my options in this case. One of my options was that of giving you no jail time at all. But I'll tell you right now I'm not going to do that." He sat back down.

Justice Allen picked up a sheaf of letters that sat in front of him. "I hold here a few of the more than 140 letters — letters from the heart — that your supporters have written. There's even one from Cardinal Egan, the archbishop of New York." The judge paused for a moment, then said, "I was touched by the letters. And in light of them, I am cutting one year off your sentence." Justice Allen gazed at the monsignor. "I therefore sentence you to serve one to four years in prison. You are to pay $50,000 in restitution in addition to what you have already paid."

Dead silence hung in the air.

Monsignor Woolsey sat like a pale statue. He couldn't believe it.

Nick DeFeis hugged him.

Finally, three minutes later, Woolsey found the energy to stand. Two bailiffs loomed behind his chair. His knees trembled as he rose. The bailiffs handcuffed him. One of them pointed toward a door to the side. As he turned, Monsignor Woolsey smiled weakly toward his supporters, who were seated together. The dazzle was gone.

The bailiffs led him out of the courtroom.

Outside the courthouse, DeFeis addressed the media. "Monsignor Woolsey is eligible for work release immediately. And I hope that he will receive it. This man should not be imprisoned. Even if he is, he will be eligible for probation within one year," said DeFeis. A quiver of irritation crisscrossed his face. He added, "I cannot think of a case where a jail sentence is less necessary. I really believe the appropriate sentence would be a sentence of community service."

His Eminence, Cardinal Edward Egan, issued the following statement only minutes after the sentencing took place. "Today's sentencing of Monsignor John Woolsey marks the end of a sad and painful period for the Parish of St. John the Martyr, the Archdiocese of New York, and Monsignor Woolsey as well. We pray that it also marks a new beginning for all who may have been hurt by or involved with this matter. With God's grace may there now be reconciliation and healing."

One year later to the day, on September 22, 2007, at 4:00 a.m., Monsignor John Woolsey walked out of the Oneida Correctional Facility. Wearing a gray sweatshirt and blue jeans, he waved and flashed a dazzling smile at reporters. He shook hands with his attorney, who greeted him as he left the prison. He didn't stop to answer questions. Instead, he headed directly to a silver SUV parked at the curb. Its motor was running, and heavily tinted windows made it impossible to see who was driving.

After the SUV roared off, Nicholas DeFeis took questions from reporters.

"Why was he released early?"

"The parole board held a hearing in July," said DeFeis. "I presented evidence of his excellent behavior while in prison and evidence of the massive amount of support he still has from his parishioners and from Cardinal Egan."

"What's he going to do now?" asked a reporter.

"That's uncertain," said DeFeis. "He has a whole life worth of good works behind him. There are lots of organizations willing to have him work as a volunteer."

While he was in prison, Monsignor Woolsey gave an interview to *The New Yorker*. When he was asked why he did what he did, Woolsey replied, "I blame my behavior on an addiction to the high life. I wish I could turn back the clock, but I can't. I feel terrible about what I've done. I feel like I'm down, and it's a dark moment in my life."

Greed is a sin. Theft is a crime. Monsignor Woolsey admitted neither. He only admitted to addiction, which implied some kind of dependency, which implied habit. According to the monsignor, it was all just a bad habit, like leaving the cap off the toothpaste tube. It was not megalomania, a mental disorder characterized by delusions of grandeur, wealth, and power.

When *The New Yorker* contacted the archdiocese about the interview, the archdiocesan spokesman made only one remark. "He's still a priest," Joseph Zwilling said. "The simple fact of going to prison does not strip him of his priesthood."

Monsignor John Woolsey is now seventy-one. He is still on probation. Whether or not he goes to hell for his sins will be decided in another court. The court of heaven at the Judgment of the Great White Throne.

# CHAPTER 4

## SERVING MAMMON

TUCKED BETWEEN THE NAVESINK RIVER and the Shrewsbury River sat the city of Rumson, in the state of New Jersey. Actually, Rumson was not a city; it was a borough. Which meant a very small town that had incorporated itself so it had the rights and privileges of a city.

Most of the people who lived in Rumson were white and Catholic. All of them were rich. The average income was $140,000. Many celebrities chose to call Rumson home. People such as Bob Ojeda, the big-league baseball pitcher; the rock stars Jon Bon Jovi and Bruce Springsteen; and Queen Latifah and Heather Locklear.

Holy Cross Roman Catholic Church was *the* church in Rumson. There were others, but Holy Cross was the oldest and the wealthiest. Lots of money dropped into the collection plates.

The pastor of Holy Cross Church was the Right Reverend William Joseph Hughes. Everybody called him Father Joe.

He was a big man, tall and overweight. His health suffered from his love of good food. Diabetes, congestive heart failure, obesity, and circulatory problems threatened to do him in on a daily basis. To keep them all at bay, he swallowed seven different medications each morning.

Even death would have to wait, because Father Joe was a busy man. Not only did he preside at weddings, funerals, and baptisms, but he also had a vision. A vision of enlarging Holy Cross Church. He wanted to double both the size of the buildings and the number of worshippers.

Taking Holy Orders in 1970, Father Joe had served at two churches in Phillipsburg, one in Middlesex, and one in Toms River. After that he had functioned as director of vocations for Warren County and then as principal of Notre Dame High School in Lawrenceville.

In 1989, the bishop of the Trenton diocese had given Father Joe a plum appointment as pastor of Holy Cross Church. Its members had lots of money, gave generously, and didn't make waves, and Rumson was a nice place to live. The people were educated, cultured, and well mannered.

The Trenton diocese required that each pastor of each church appoint a lay committee to oversee his church's money. Which meant that they — the committee — set spending priorities and managed the parish's money.

According to Father Hughes, lay committees were a joke. They never agreed on anything. And they never got anything done. All they did do was get in the way. Father Hughes had other plans.

Once he arrived at Holy Cross, he did not appoint any committees. He was in charge, and he made the decisions. End of discussion. He didn't bluster and bully. He just quietly went ahead and did what he wanted to do. Without consulting anyone.

One thing Father Joe wanted to do was live well. Surrounded by conspicuous consumption, he wanted to consume too. In his first year at Holy Cross, he skimmed $43,000 from the collection plates.

Holy Cross held a number of bank accounts, and Father Joe controlled them all. To avoid detection, he simply opened another bank account at a different bank. The bank he chose was in the nearby borough of Sea Bright, an aptly named place right by the Atlantic Ocean with plenty of sunshine. Every Tuesday or Wednesday he would drive over and deposit cash in his account. It was easy.

Father Joe had a twin brother named Thomas. While they were growing up in the Irish Catholic enclave of East Keansburg, the twins were very close. Thomas dreamed of being a millionaire when he grew up, while William Joseph wanted to be a priest. He didn't know exactly why he wanted to be a priest. But it seemed like a good thing. People respected priests.

Thomas's dream came true, and Joseph got what he wanted. Thomas started small, opening a concession stand on the boardwalk in Atlantic City, New Jersey. It did well. So he opened another one, then another one, then more and more. Until he owned a chain of them. The money rolled in.

Eager to invest, Thomas plunked his money into hotels on the boardwalk. He bought the older ones, fixed them up, changed the names, and put in some slots. His hotels catered to the low- to middle-income people who, when they came to Atlantic City, wanted a cheap place to stay. The money rolled in.

Then in 1990, shortly after Father Joe took over Holy Cross Church, Thomas dropped dead. He was only forty-seven. But his heart was bad.

After attorney fees and the cost of the funeral, there was a lot of money in the estate. Thomas left most of it to his twin brother; the rest went to their mother.

On the one hand, Thomas's death shocked Father Joe. Thomas seemed too young to die, but he did. Father Joe understood — once and for all — how short life really was and how precarious it was. Anyone could go at anytime. So Father Joe decided to make the best of whatever time he had left. "Live life like you mean it" became his motto.

Also, grimly, the timing couldn't have been better. Father Joe wanted to buy some toys with the stolen $43,000 but hadn't because people would start to wonder where a priest got so much money. When Thomas died, Father Joe dropped some hints around Rumson. The rich brother had passed away, leaving his money to the priest. Even though stricken by grief at his loss, Father Joe somehow found the energy to start spending.

He bought himself a BMW and had a six-person hot tub installed on the back patio of the rectory. Health reasons were given as excuses. Father Joe was a big man and required a car that was easy to get in and out of. And the hot tub stimulated his body's circulation and helped him to sweat out toxins. Both the hot tub and the BMW were top of the line. When Father Joe soaked in the hot tub, he felt pampered. When he drove his BMW, he felt important, as if he was somebody.

Thomas had owned a condominium in Florida, which now belonged to Father Joe. Joe didn't want the property as Florida wasn't his kind of place. So he arranged to sell it.

Sitting in his office at Holy Cross, Father Joe made a call

to Jay Harbeck. Jay was an investment banker and a member of the church. Sometimes the two men had lunch together. "Jay," said Father Joe. "How are you?"

"I'm well, Father, but awfully busy today. What can I do for you?" Harbeck liked the priest. He was charismatic, looked out for the needy, and had a nice "touch" with the Sunday mass.

"Well," said Father Joe, "my brother recently passed on, and he left me a piece of property down in Florida."

"I heard you had inherited some money," said Jay. Then, by way of explanation, he added, "Rumson's a small place, you know? Things get around."

"I know," said Father Joe, smiling. "Anyway, the place in Florida isn't feasible right now. I have too many duties and responsibilities here. And I'm never going to use the place. What do you suggest?"

"Rent it or sell it," said Jay.

"Which would you advise?"

"If you rent it, you have the hassle of maintaining it," said Jay. "Of course, you can always hire some property management firm to do that for you. But even that presents some problems."

"And selling it?"

"Other than taxes, it's a good time to sell. The market for houses is up. And, of course, you're going to have to pay taxes no matter what," said Jay.

"That's what I thought," agreed Father Joe. "But I wanted an expert's take on it." He paused, pretending to think about it. "Yeah, I think I'll just go ahead and sell it. Do you know anyone down south who could handle it for me?"

"Sure thing," said Jay. "I'll give a call down to him. His name is Saul — Saul Jonas. I'll have him call you in a day or two. You'll like him. He's a real pro and will get you top dollar for the place."

"Excellent," said Father Joe. "That's just excellent. Thanks, Jay. And hey, let's do dinner soon. My treat."

Saul Jonas called two days later. He agreed to list and handle the sale of the condominium.

Two weeks later it sold. Some developer snapped it up at the asking price. An easy $200,000. When the check arrived, Father Joe got in his new Beemer and drove over to Sea Bright, where he deposited the money in his checking account.

On the way back to Rumson, he decided to take a vacation. Some place warm with beaches where they served multicolored exotic drinks with little umbrellas in them. He would get a tan and read some novels. Thrillers and murder mysteries were his favorites.

Back in his office at Holy Cross, Father Joe called his travel agent. She suggested Cancun. Even the name was exotic.

"Sounds great," said Father Joe. "Book me a first-class flight and a suite in a five-star hotel."

"How soon do you want to leave?" she asked.

"In two weeks," he said without hesitation. "And I'll be there for ten days."

"Okay," she said and hung up.

Except for the fact that he lusted for material things, Father Joe took his job seriously. He liked helping people. The act of giving to others gave him goosebumps — a kind of tingly satisfaction.

He felt driven to help someone. Rummaging through his mind, he searched for someone to help. Problem was there weren't many poor people in Rumson. Everybody drove

Beemers and Benzes and wore J. Crew outfits out on their thirty-foot sailboats. A notion bubbled and fizzed in his brain.

David Rogers, who worked for the church as a jack-of-all-trades, kept the grounds up, maintained the building, cleaned, and swept. He was a glorified janitor. Holy Cross Church paid Rogers $50,000 a year for his services, which wasn't bad really. But in an area where people spent that much every year on French wines for their basement wine cellars, well, it didn't go far.

David lived in an apartment in the nearby township of Howell. He lived there for two reasons. One, Rumson didn't have any apartments for rent. All Rumson had were million-dollar estates. Two, if Rumson had had any apartments, the rent would be $5,000 per month, more than David even made.

Father Joe decided that David was perfect. Learning disabled, David would never be much more than a janitor. And since he was only twenty-five, he had a lengthy purgatory of janitorial work ahead of him. But with Father Joe's help, maybe life wouldn't be so bad. The prospect of helping someone gave Father Joe that warm feeling.

Smiling and happy, he went to find David. No doubt he was around the church somewhere. He found him in the sanctuary. David was spraying Liquid Gold on the altar, then buffing it by hand with a soft rag.

"David," said Father Joe, moving his hefty weight around slowly.

"Yes, Father?" said David, still buffing. He gazed intently at the dark wood of the altar, watching it take on a sheen.

"When you finish with that, I'd like for you to come with me. Over to Sea Bright."

Looking up, David said, "Sure thing, Father. Just a few more minutes and I'll be done here."

Fifteen minutes later Father Joe and David Rogers were in the brand-new BMW blasting along the tarmac.

"Nice car, Father," said David, glancing around the interior. He rubbed the gray leather of his seat.

"It is, isn't it?" agreed Father Joe, smiling with pleasure. Another idea materialized as if someone had flicked a Bic in his brain. "Would you like to have a car like this?" said Father Joe.

"Boy, would I!"

"Well, when I get back from my vacation, David, why don't you and I go car shopping?"

"I don't have enough money for one of these, Father," said David. He laughed. "I couldn't even pay for the insurance on a car like this."

"Sure you could," said Father Joe. "If someone helped you."

David squinted at him. "What do you mean, Father?"

"What I mean is this," said Father Joe. His big grin looked like a banana was stuck sideways in his mouth. "I'm going to buy you one."

David peered at him. "Why?"

Father Joe laughed. "Because I want to, David. And because you deserve it."

David shrugged. "Okay," he said simply. "Thanks."

As they drove along, Father Joe decided that being learning disabled might be better than being normal. A normal person would have inquired about his motives, wondered where he got the money, or possibly refused. Not David, he just accepted it and said thanks. There was something clean and healthy about that.

Arriving at Sea Bright, Father Joe drove to Circuit City. He parked the new BMW at an angle, taking up two spaces. He didn't want it to get scratched.

Once inside the store, Father Joe asked David two questions. What did he need? And what did he want?

David needed a new refrigerator. So they picked out a stainless steel one. Made by Sub-Zero, it was top of the line and had all the latest doo-dads: filtered water dispenser, ice dispenser, and a digital thermometer readout. That way David would know how cold his food was, Father Joe justified flimsily. David wanted a big-screen television. He selected a Sony with a 52" monitor.

Father Joe paid cash. The two items would be delivered the next day, and installation was part of the package. Father Joe wasn't sure David could read and follow the instruction booklets.

Zooming back to Rumson, Father Joe had another amazing insight. Going to Cancun alone didn't sound like much fun. So why not take David? He was sure David had never been anywhere outside New Jersey. It would be a new experience for him. And company for Father Joe.

"David?"

"Yes, Father?"

"How'd you like to go to Cancun?"

"Fine, Father," said David. "As long as it doesn't take too long. I want to get back and finish the altar this afternoon."

Father Joe roared with laughter. David didn't even know where Cancun was.

"It's a resort in Mexico, David," said Father Joe patiently. "A place where people go for vacation. There's swimming and water-skiing and hang-gliding. All sorts of fun things to do." He glanced at David. "Would you like to go?"

David shrugged. "Sure. As soon as I finish polishing the altar, I'll be ready."

Father Joe laughed again. This would be fun.

When Father Joe and David returned from Cancun, they were tanned and rested. David brought back a large straw sombrero with red-and-yellow stitching on the crown. He put it on and went out to mow the lawns that surrounded Holy Cross Church. Usually, he mowed the lawns once a week. Twelve days without grooming had left the grass shaggy looking, like a green sheepdog.

In Cancun, Father Joe had eaten too much, washing the food down with vast amounts of alcohol. His blood sugar was shot to hell. Using his diabetic test kit every hour, he was slapped in the face by the numbers. He needed to get his life under control.

Instead, he wrote a check from Holy Cross payable to cash, then drove his BMW over to Sea Bright and deposited the check. His personal checking account swelled by $100,000. Having a lot of money in the bank made him feel in control.

Back in Rumson, he pulled up in front of Holy Cross Church and, leaving the German engine growling, went looking for David. Finding him in the garage, Father Joe told him to drop what he was doing. They were going car shopping.

David washed his greasy hands and galloped out to the BMW. Because he had taken to wearing his sombrero at all times, David had a hard time wedging into the car. Once he was in, Father Joe floored it. The car trailing gravel like a rooster tail, Father Joe watched as Holy Cross Church receded in his rearview mirror.

Arriving in Trenton, they drove to the Porsche dealership, which sat on car row, a wide boulevard at the north end of town. Driving along car row was like taking cocaine. It provided a buzzing, lust-filled high, a kind of heavy-metal fix.

David, it turned out, knew what kind of car he wanted. He just didn't know what brand it was. He had seen the car in an action movie. Red and swept back, it had a funny-sounding name, like someone sneezing. After some quizzing, Father Joe determined that the sneezing sound was a Porsche.

At the Porsche dealership, Father Joe and David strolled through the gleaming cars. David spotted a red one and ran to it. This was the one. Just like in the movie.

Father Joe insisted they test-drive the car, even though David just wanted to buy it. After the test drive, Father Joe told the salesman, "Wrap it up. We'll take it." He didn't haggle over the price. Just wrote out a check for $41,238.21.

David, who had never driven a stick shift before, bucked out of the lot, heading for the turnpike. He still wore his sombrero. Father Joe followed behind like a mother hen guiding a wayward chick.

Also around this time, Father Joe moved his mother into the spare room at the rectory. He spent nearly ten grand fixing the room up. Painters gave the room a fresh green coat, a technician installed a big-screen television in the corner, and a bed with 600-thread-count sheets was delivered.

Cancer was eating his mother from the inside out. The doctor's prognosis was bad. A few months, at most a few years. Father Joe prayed for her, lit candles, even said the sacrament for the sick over her. Finally, he anointed her with holy oil. It had come from Jerusalem and been blessed by a rabbi. According to the Roman Catholic Church, this was heresy. Father Joe didn't care. He just wanted his mother to live.

She died in 1997. Father Joe said mass for her. As he left the cemetery, a snowy loneliness settled on him, oozing into his bones. It never went away. Trying to forget it, he went crazy. Not the kind of craziness he could be committed for but the kind where he searched frantically for something to fill up the emptiness. There was a big hole inside him.

.  Father Joe tried to stuff the hole with things. He bought David Rogers a house in a quiet neighborhood in the township of Howell. It cost only $200,000. Father Joe put $40,000 down on it and began making the monthly mortgage payments. Then he sent David on vacation to the exclusive Elbow Beach Club in Bermuda.

Father Joe didn't neglect himself. He purchased season tickets to the New York Giants home football games. He traveled in style to the games. Leaving his BMW parked at the church, he chartered a stretch limo from Arrow Limousine Service. On the trips to New York, he sat in the back sipping Irish whiskey or wine. He felt special.

.  When the game ended, Father Joe spent the night at the Waldorf Astoria in the Big Apple. He took a suite and ordered room service. Sometimes he attended Broadway shows, always with a seat in the first three rows. He liked musical comedies the best. Upbeat and lighthearted, the singing and jesting smothered the gloomy thoughts that visited him. He didn't know it, but tons of guilt pressed on him like a great boulder of granite.

When the weekend was over, Father Joe took the limo back to Rumson. In his kitchen at the rectory, he displayed the playbills from the shows he had seen. He stuck them on the walls. There were a lot of them. When he looked at them, they reminded him that he had done something, enjoyed something — that he had a life. They declared that the sum of his life was more than saying mass and listening to confessions.

Then in 2000 things started to go to hell.

Father Joe was determined to expand Holy Cross Church. The plans he submitted to the Rumson zoning board included doubling the size of the sanctuary, which already seated 300. A gymnasium would be built, and classrooms would be added to the Holy Cross School, which was fifty years old.

Holy Cross School was one of two private schools in Rumson. The other school, Rumson Country Day School, did not have any religious affiliation. Competition for students was fierce but unspoken. Since money wasn't a factor in Rumson, the more robust a school looked, the better its chances of attracting pupils. Image was everything in a place where money was everywhere.

The proposed improvements split the members of Holy Cross Church down the middle. Holy Cross became a house divided against itself.

Those against the idea were the most vocal. They thought it was extravagant and unnecessary. It would cost too much money and destroy the quaintness of the 120-year-old sanctuary. And Rumson, with its old money, old mansions, and old ways, was all about quaintness and tradition. Anything that smacked of change was spawned by the devil.

The members behind the expansion said it was time to "move forward." They avoided the dreadful word *change*. Holy Cross needed to become a modern church if it wanted to attract young new members.

Rumson's zoning board rejected the plans.

Father Joe was pissed off. He made an appointment to see Mayor John E. Ekdahl, a tall, distinguished man who just happened to be a member of Holy Cross. The two men sat in the mayor's office.

"What's the deal, John?" said Father Joe, shifting his bulk in his chair. "How come the zoning board blew my plans out of the water?"

Mayor Ekdahl raised his hands, pressing against the priest's angry energy. "I know you're upset, Father Joe. But look, this is a volatile issue. People feel strongly about it. Maybe we can reach some sort of compromise."

"No," said Father Joe. "It's just politics, and you know it. There is no convincing reason why Holy Cross should not be allowed to expand. Except the old fuddie-duddies don't want it." He snorted in disgust.

"You're right," said Mayor Ekdahl. "It is definitely a political issue." He glanced down at his desk, then back at the priest. "Since you brought it up, I'll tell you exactly what some people are thinking," said the mayor.

Father Joe nodded. "Okay. Let's hear it."

"Well, some people think — and I'm one of them — that you're merely doing what the diocese over in Trenton has instructed you to do. That because of shrinking congregations, a shortage of priests, higher maintenance costs for all the church properties, and all the recent lawsuits for sexual abuse — the diocese wants to consolidate things. Bring the smaller churches together into one bigger church — the church in Rumson," spelled out the mayor.

"People who believe that are sadly mistaken," said Father Joe. "The expansion of Holy Cross was my idea. I presented it to the diocese, and they approved it. But other than okaying it, they have nothing to do with it."

Mayor Ekdahl nodded.

"And as far as I know," continued Father Joe, "all the shore parishes are healthy. Numbers are up, both in members and finances. There is no reason for the diocese to consolidate. Everything's fine."

"Well, some people don't see it that way," said the mayor, cocking his head skeptically. He leaned forward a little. "Some people think the diocese told you to shake the money tree here in Rumson and expand Holy Cross and the school."

Father Joe's eyebrows came together in surprise. Then the priest put his head back and laughed. "Now that I believe," he said, chuckling. "In Rumson the reason is always money because they're all afraid they're going to run out of it."

Mayor Ekdahl smiled and shrugged in half-hearted agreement.

Father Joe shifted his heavy body and leaned to the side. "Holy Cross will be expanded, John. One way or the other," he said in a fat voice.

"Now, Joe," said the mayor, raising his hands for peace. "Don't get all heavyhanded about this. Give me a little time. I'll see what I can do. But to be honest, I'm against it myself. I don't see a need for it."

Father Joe stared at the mayor for a few seconds. "You're entitled to your opinion." He hesitated as if holding something back. "Thanks for your time."

As the priest left, Mayor Ekdahl wondered what Father Joe would do now.

Father Joe became heavyhanded.

He hired an attorney, one from Trenton. The guy was a good Catholic and an expert in zoning regulations. The attorney filed a lawsuit, which cited an obscure federal law that had been passed that year. The law, designed to protect fringe religious groups, said that discrimination against churches applying for rezoning violated religious freedom. It existed to ensure the religious freedom of so-called cults. It was never meant to be used by large, mainline denominations such as the Roman Catholics, but the attorney grabbed hold of it and began swinging it like Samson fighting the Philistines with the jawbone of an ass. Get out of the way, or get cut down.

The Philistines hired their own attorney.

After a while, though, common sense got in the way of a knock-down, drag-out fight.

The zoning board admitted they would lose if the matter went before a judge. No judge in the land would rule against religious freedom, especially the freedom of the Catholic Church, especially in an area that was predominantly Catholic.

After much arguing back and forth, a settlement was reached out of court. Holy Cross got permission to expand — but only half as much as it had wanted. The sanctuary, which seated 300, could grow to seat 450. And the school could be enlarged — but only by half of what had originally been asked for. The zoning board insisted that ample parking be provided and that all architectural plans be approved beforehand by the board.

The zoning board got its revenge too. A construction performance bond had to be posted before any work began. Which meant Holy Cross had to come up with a bundle of cash to be held in escrow. In other words, the church had to raise twice as much money as it needed. Enough for the bond and enough to pay for the construction itself. Legally, the zoning board could require such a bond without risking another lawsuit. So they did, hoping that it would foil Father Joe's grandiose plans.

It didn't. Father Joe just kept shaking the Rumson money tree.

Meanwhile, Father Joe kept skimming money from the collection plates. He bought two more new BMWs: one for David Rogers, who was getting bored with the red Porsche, and one for himself.

Father Joe continued to travel to New York City for his weekends of Broadway plays, expensive restaurants, and luxury hotel suites. And later he too took a vacation to Bermuda. He flew first-class and stayed at a swank island resort, where he worked on his tan, drank sugary drinks, and had a daily massage.

Father Joe threw a party for himself on his sixtieth birthday. The party took place at Sea Bright Country Club. Invitations went out, mostly to members of Holy Cross Church. Father Joe said it was his way of celebrating his life and the generosity of his parishioners. They had contributed a lot of money for the church expansion.

Superb food, prepared by the club's French chef, and an open bar were provided. A jazz band played upbeat songs. Father Joe smiled and laughed as he greeted his guests and friends. He drank too much and ate too much. But it was his birthday, so what the heck?

Father Joe paid $25,000 in church cash for the party. His guests didn't know and never suspected they were footing the bill for everything, including Father Joe's glamorous lifestyle.

Life was sweetest for Father Joe right before things turned sour.

Holy Cross became a money pit. Inside the pit lived a monster with an insatiable appetite. Massive amounts of money were poured into the pit every day. Church expansion was not cheap.

Because of the sums involved, the Diocese of Trenton decided that fiscal responsibility was its new watchword. To make sure of it, the diocese ordered a routine audit of the books at Holy Cross. The church didn't need any more scandals. So a swarm of accountants jammed into the offices at Holy Cross Church. They began poring over the numbers. Since Father Joe was the bookkeeper, if any questions arose, they went to him.

One day one of the accountants stumbled across an unknown bank account. It had been opened in 1997, and a lot of money had been funneled into it. Money from church accounts. This curious information was reported to the bishop, who ordered an extensive investigation. A routine audit had just turned into a number-crunching version of the Spanish Inquisition.

No one said anything to Father Joe. He thought everything was just fine. As soon as the accountants left, he could get back to his normal way of life. He hoped they would hurry. He was planning a vacation in a few months, probably to Bermuda again. But he was also considering Europe. From what all the rich people in town said, it must be nice.

The accountants discovered that the monthly statements for the unknown account didn't come to the church. Instead, they went to a post office box in the town of Sea Bright. This was bad. The statements showed that at least $500,000 had been deposited into the unknown account.

When the bishop heard the amount, he almost fainted. Immediately, he ordered the findings turned over to the Monmouth County prosecutor. On the phone, the bishop told Robert Honecker, Jr., the first assistant Monmouth County prosecutor, "We have determined by means of an internal audit that Father Hughes is involved in financial irregularities — a misappropriation of funds. We believe, because of the amount involved, that it is criminal in nature."

"Where are the records?" asked Honecker.

"They are on their way to you even as we speak," said the bishop.

"Good," said Honecker. "I'll have our forensic account-ants get right on it." He hung up.

Six months later the bishop asked his secretary to dial a number.

"Yes," said Father Joe, answering his office phone at Holy Cross.

"Joseph?" said a voice.

Father Joe recognized the tone of the bishop. "Yes," he said. He had a feeling the jig was up. There was a sinking sensa-tion in his chest, as if his heart had plunged into his stomach.

"Joseph," said the bishop in a stern tone. "Because of cer-tain irregularities — financial irregularities — I am asking for your resignation as pastor of Holy Cross. In addition, I am removing all your priestly privileges."

Stunned, Father Joe didn't answer. He felt as if someone had just pulled the plugs from the soles of his feet, draining out all his blood.

"Joseph? Do you understand what I said?"

"Yes." Father Joe hung up.

Like a hunk of marble, he sat motionless for a few min-utes. Then he reached for the Yellow Pages. Flipping through to L, he found Lawyers. He used his finger, running down the page to a subheading. Criminal Defense Lawyers. Reaching for his cell phone, he dialed a number.

"Law offices," answered a female voice on the other end.

"May I speak with Mr. Pappa?" said Father Joe.

"One moment, please. I'll connect you," said the woman.

"This is Michael Pappa," said a rumbling voice.

"Hello. My name is Father Joseph Hughes. I'm the pastor — rather, I was the pastor — of Holy Cross. I need help."

"Relax, Father," said Pappa. "Why don't you come to my office? We'll talk about it and see what we can do. How's that sound?"

"When?"

"Right away," said Pappa. "I'll be waiting for you. Fortunately, I don't have court this afternoon."

"I'm leaving now," said Father Joe. He hung up, grabbed the keys to his BMW, and walked out of Holy Cross for the last time.

Later that afternoon all his personal belongings were moved out of the rectory. A truck took them to a diocesan retreat house — Father Joe's new home while events unraveled. It was November 1, 2004.

Meanwhile, at the end of a six-month grand jury investigation, an indictment was handed down. Honecker issued a warrant for the arrest of Father Joseph Hughes.

On November 4, 2004, Father Joe turned himself in to the Rumson Police Department. His attorney was with him. Father Joe was charged with three counts of grand theft. The police took his fingerprints and put him in a holding cell until his arraignment.

His arraignment took place two days later. After pleading not guilty, his bail was set at $100,000. He posted bail, and his attorney drove him back to the retreat house.

The next day the Prosecutor's Office stated that Father Hughes, now sixty, used a credit card to purchase $52,000 worth of airline tickets, along with lavish dinners at expensive restaurants and other personal expenses. Those expenses included stays at various Marriott Hotels in New Jersey and

Florida.

Money to pay off the credit card came from Holy Cross Church. The money was in an investment account at Merrill Lynch. Father Joe had transferred funds from the Merrill Lynch account into the unknown account — his account.

The police also determined that Father Hughes used an additional $100,000 from the investment account to purchase gifts for David Rogers. Gifts included the $58,000 BMW, a Porsche, the stainless steel refrigerator, jewelry, a big-screen television, and the mortgage and utility payments on a house in Howell. They found out about all of it.

"We went to Arrow Limousine Service," said an investigator, "and they confirmed that Father Hughes spent a little over $50,000 for trips back and forth to New York City, to airports, restaurants, and Broadway shows."

He also spent $397,000 on other "personal expenses." This money came from the unknown account in Sea Bright. The money in the account had been transferred from Holy Cross accounts. Checks payable to "cash" had been used to make the transfers. Father Joe's signature was on the checks.

David Rogers was not charged. But the police described him as a person of interest and would question him as soon as possible. "I don't believe he was unwitting," Honecker said. "The issue to be determined is if he was aware if the funds being utilized were church funds or were they personal funds of the reverend." Rogers was indeed unwitting. The police discovered after questioning him that he had a learning disability. It was obvious. They didn't need any experts to confirm it.

About Father Hughes, Honecker said, "I don't think anyone in the community had an idea, including the local law enforcement, that the church funds were substantially being used to subsidize his lifestyle." According to Honecker, Father Hughes had inherited a large sum of money from his brother, and many parishioners assumed it was that money, and not parish funds, that provided Father Hughes with his luxurious lifestyle.

When interviewed, parishioners of Holy Cross Church gave their candid opinions. Shocked and dismayed, a few church members were faultfinding and backbiting. Most demonstrated a peculiar type of sympathy for Father Joe, probably because the love of money was nothing new to them.

Rosemary Hulse expressed her disappointment. "It's like he went bananas when he saw all the money in Rumson," said the seventy-seven-year-old Rosemary. "I can't imagine a priest doing this. I thought they committed no sin, but I have certainly changed my opinion." Rosemary had been born and raised in Rumson and came from old money. She also seemed to be looking at priests through Norman Rockwell sunglasses — the kind that made priests pure.

A local merchant who spoke only when guaranteed that his name wouldn't be mentioned said there had been whispered gossip about Father Joe's lavish lifestyle — lots of vacations, the hot tub, and the BMW. "Those people complaining had four more like his back home in their driveways," jeered the merchant. "You have to keep these things in perspective."

Linda Davies thought Father Joe was a nice guy. "He was a priest foremost," she said, "and he had a gift and a charisma that brought people into the church." Linda understood, kind of. She, too, came from a blue-collar background. Putting herself in his skin, she imagined he might have had a secret longing for the high life. Hastily, she added that Father Joe never allowed the gaudy display of Rumson to blind him to the "tear in a parishioner's eye."

Stephen Sheehan remarked that Father Hughes conducted a beautiful mass and had a touch that made him wonder about the fancy BMW and the craving for creature comforts.

Jay Harbeck, the investment banker, also had an opinion. He thought Father Joe was "lonely." And that loneliness explained a lot of human failings.

Father Joe had many supporters who declared that he used the stolen money to help those in need. Which meant he didn't really steal the money. He just redirected it.

But John Kaye, the Monmouth County prosecutor, pooh-poohed that idea. "This was all to support his lifestyle," said Kaye. "This man probably did a lot of good for people because his job puts him in that position. But people commit theft because they think they will get away with it."

Michael Pappa, Father Joe's defense attorney, tried to get the court to impose a gag order. He thought that all the gossip and wild speculation did nothing but damage his client's right to a fair hearing. One-sided ideas poisoned any potential jurors. He didn't want to deal with that.

The court threw out his first motion for the gag order. Later Pappa submitted another motion, and the court accepted it. Everyone was told to keep his or her mouth shut. Which meant prosecutors, defense attorneys, and all law enforcement officers.

Near the end of the court hearing, Pappa drove to the nearby township of Long Branch, where Father Joe was living in the retreat house. The lawyer sat down with the priest and gave him his options.

The retreat house sat near the beach. It was a large, rambling structure built of wood. Painted white with blue trim, it was well maintained. Inside, though, Pappa found the furnishings severe. No big-screen television, no leather couches, and no comfy chairs. But that was to be expected in a religious retreat.

"These are our advantages if you decide to take it to trial," said Pappa. "First off, they have to prove criminal intent. Which will be hard to do. If you gave the money away, who's to say that that is theft or a crime?"

Father Joe sat quietly, listening. Still shaken by his indictment and arrest, he had been comforting himself by eating. So his weight was up, which was bad. But right now he really didn't care.

"Will a jury buy that?" he asked.

Pappa answered truthfully. "Maybe," he said. "And I say maybe because there's a murkiness that exists. There are no set standards. Canon law allows for pastors to give money in charity — to parishioners in time of need. And you have self-entitlement — you can use it for personal needs."

"But can we prove that?"

Pappa shook his head. "We can. But probably not to the satisfaction of the court or a jury," he said.

"So where does that leave me?" asked Father Joe. "I mean, what's my other option?"

"You plead guilty," said Pappa.

Father Joe paled. Sweat beaded on his forehead.

"It's not as bad as it sounds," said Pappa in a soothing tone. "I'll talk to the prosecutors. Tell them we want a plea bargain. You'll plead guilty to one or two charges, the others will be dropped, and then you'll have to do some time in jail."

"How much time?"

"I can't say for sure," said Pappa. "But not much. And — there's all sorts of ways to reduce that."

Father Joe thought about this. Finally, he said, "Okay. I guess we bargain."

Pappa smiled. "I'll talk to the prosecutors as soon as I get back to my office. Hang tight. This'll all be over soon, and then you can get on with your life."

Father Joe shook his head and made a whiffing sound.

Criminal investigations take time. Plea bargains take even more time.

On May 4, 2006, sixty-two-year-old Father Joe stood with his attorney in state Superior Court in Freehold, New Jersey. Father Joe was there to plead guilty.

This was the deal: he would plead guilty to three counts. One count of theft by deception, one count of filing a fraudulent tax return, and one count of failure to pay state income tax. The rest of the charges would be dismissed by the Prosecutor's Office. All together Father Joe was charged with twenty-seven counts, all felonies. So, all in all, it was a pretty good deal. But Father Joe lacked perspective since he was the one who had to go to prison.

During the proceedings, Father Joe said only one word. When the judge asked him how he pled, he said, "Guilty."

A shiver ran through the packed courtroom.

The prosecutor rose and said that he recommended a sentence of five years in prison.

The judge nodded but didn't comment. Then she said, "Sentencing will take place on June 2, 2006."

Pappa drove Father Joe back to the retreat house. On the way, Father Joe had a question. "What sentence do you think

I'll get?"

Pappa looked uncomfortable. "Probably that recommended by the prosecutor," he said. "But before you despair, remember what I told you. Once you're in prison, you immediately apply for the Intensive Supervision Program. Once accepted, you do what they tell you, and you'll be out in less than a year. Guaranteed."

"You're sure about this?" said Father Joe.

"Absolutely," replied Pappa.

June 2, 2006. Freehold, New Jersey, the state Superior Court. Judge Bette Uhrmacher presiding.

"Your Honor," said Michael Pappa, "my client would like to make a statement before he is sentenced."

Judge Uhrmacher nodded. "Go ahead."

Father Joe rose from his chair. He wore a dark suit and a white cotton shirt without a tie. He sweated with embarrassment. Fear clogged his throat.

"I betrayed the trust of the people, the trust they placed in me, and I am truly sorry. I am sorry for the hurt I caused my family, my friends, and most especially the people of Holy Cross, who I love.

"My gift has always been to give, and I have given too much, and it has taken a toll on me personally. And in the aftermath of the terrorist attacks on New York City, my emotional stress increased. My way of dealing with that stress was to give, and Holy Cross Church was the victim of this.

"I ask terribly for forgiveness. I can't tell you how regretful I am."

Judge Uhrmacher nodded, looking down at her notes. "Father Hughes," she said, "I have taken note of your many good deeds. And I have read with interest the many letters written in your behalf. I also received letters from parishioners who believe you should serve time for your crimes. It makes this even sadder that this is now a divided congregation." Raising her head, she looked at Father Joe. "But on the whole," she said, "the needs of justice require that your lavish and excessive spending — which corroded the faith and trust of your church — be punished."

Father Joe blinked and gave a tight nod.

"You were not meeting the needs of the needy in this case," Judge Uhrmacher told him. "You were meeting the needs of the greedy and serving yourself." She then said, "I sentence you to five years in prison. You will serve that time in a minimum-security facility in the state of New Jersey."

The judge remanded Father Joe to jail. The bailiffs were instructed to take charge of him.

The two tax-related felonies demanded three years each. Felony grand theft demanded five years. All three of the sentences would run concurrently, which meant that Father Joe could serve all three at the same time. They would not be added on top of each other. So instead of eleven years, he would do five years.

Additionally, Father Joe agreed to what was called restitution. He had to pay back $2,032,422 along with $122,000 in state taxes. But everyone knew it probably would never happen.

It was all part of the deal negotiated by Pappa.

Outside the courtroom, two informal press conferences were held: one by Michael Pappa, and one by the Prosecutor's Office.

Over on Pappa's side of the hallway, a reporter asked about a rumor he had heard. "There's been a report that the church has offered to pay back the $2 million," said the reporter. "Is that true?"

"In the past," said Pappa, "some parishioners offered to raise funds to pay that debt. But it was conditional, based on no jail time for Father Hughes. So after he serves his time, Father Hughes will have to get a job to pay back the money. His wages will undoubtedly be garnished for that purpose."

Later, when Stephen Sheehan heard about the rumored offer, he told reporters that he was not surprised. He explained that the people making the offer had generous hearts and that Father Joe was very well liked. Then he added, "Plus, $2 million is chump change in this town." Sheehan was not only a straight shooter but also entertaining.

A reporter asked Pappa if he thought the sentence of five years was fair.

"Let me answer that question by saying this," said Pappa. "Second-degree theft is a crime that presumes jail time. However, there are mitigating circumstances which should have kept Father Hughes out of jail."

"What mitigating circumstances are you referring to?" asked the same reporter, taking notes rapidly.

"Father Hughes' health is rapidly failing," said Pappa. "He suffers diabetes, congestive heart failure, and has limited cardiovascular functions. These are all chronic health conditions."

His tone of voice implied that Father Hughes had just received a death sentence.

"There is also the issue of canon law," said Pappa. "The laws that govern the Catholic Church allow for pastors to have absolute discretion on how church funds are spent."

"So you're saying he's not guilty?" asked another reporter. A skeptical look clouded his face.

"A murkiness exists because there are no set standards," Pappa explained. "And canon law allows for pastors to give money to parishioners in time of need. And they also have what is called priestly entitlements. Those entitlements account for most, if not all, of the unaccounted for funds."

"How do you mean?"

"Like David Rogers, for example," said Pappa. "Here's David Rogers who Father Hughes met at a church conference in Florida. The man's plight tore at Father Hughes' heart. He was in need. Father Hughes believed that Rogers would become homeless and unemployed if he took away his help. Father Hughes admits that this help was inappropriate, excessive, and beyond what is acceptable under canon law."

"Yeah, but what about his BMW?" scoffed a reporter.

Pappa looked insulted. "Father Hughes acknowledges that he treated himself very well with nice dinners and Broadway shows," said Pappa. "But he was entitled to day-to-day expenses. Father Hughes did not have a cook, therefore he was entitled to go out to eat." Pappa stared at the reporters. "Father Hughes' philosophy was to help the needy. Unfortunately, he did not use generally accepted accounting principles in his work."

"Well, if that's the case, then why did he plead guilty?" asked a reporter.

"He chose to plead guilty and take responsibility," said Pappa, a talented spin-doctor.

Over at the other informal press conference, John F. Loughrey and Luis Valentin took questions from reporters. Loughrey was the assistant prosecutor. Valentin was the prosecutor.

"What about the canon law defense?" asked a reporter.

Valentin explained that, if the case had gone to trial, he

would have argued that canon law was not applicable. "Our evidence in this case and our legal research finds no canon law to defend what crimes were committed by Father Hughes. We would have submitted legal briefs that this should not have been considered," Valentin said.

Loughrey added that there was no proof that Father Hughes had given any of the $2 million to help anyone. "We can see check by check by check," said Loughrey, "what Father Hughes spent, what he spent it on, and who he spent it on."

"What other evidence is there? That Father Hughes spent all the money on himself?" asked a reporter from the Freehold newspaper.

Valentin nodded to Loughrey to answer the question. Loughrey had worked with the forensic accountants, so he knew his stuff.

"The church bookkeeper told our investigators that Father Hughes would count the Sunday mass collection money privately, counting only the large bills and depositing the money himself on Mondays and Tuesdays," said Loughrey. He paused and shrugged. Then he admitted, "That's circumstantial, but a pastor is not supposed to count the collection money from Sunday. He didn't think it was necessary because he wanted to have control over everything." Holding up his hand to yield a point, Loughrey said, "I do not dispute Mr. Pappas' claims that Father Hughes was a good priest — a claim which is supported by the letters the judge referred to. But I believe jail time is appropriate in this case." Then Loughrey summed it all up. "This fall from grace for him is stark and bitter and devastating," he said, "but he has only himself to blame."

The Prosecutor's Office handed out a press release. "The

comprehensive audit revealed that during the eight years covered in the indictment, Hughes wrote out and endorsed nearly half a million dollars in checks made payable to 'cash' against five church bank accounts. Hughes additionally wrote $1.4 million in checks against Holy Cross Church accounts to cover unauthorized personal expenses. Neither Holy Cross Church nor its parishioners received any benefit from these unauthorized expenditures."

Father Michael Manning was appointed as pastor of Holy Cross Church. He would replace Father Joe, who was on his way to prison.

"I will pray for Father Hughes and for those harmed by his theft," said Father Manning. "The facts hurt but eventually will hasten the healing already begun and promote an atmosphere of openness and honesty in the parish."

Later in the afternoon on the day he was sentenced to five years in prison, sixty-two-year-old Father Joseph Hughes entered Burlington County Prison.

Inmate processing there took four hours. Father Joe received prison-issued clothing, prison-issued shoes, and prison-issued ID. After being fingerprinted, he was interviewed by medical personnel. An interview by a prison official followed. Finally, they gave him a bedroll — two sheets and a blanket — and placed him in a lockdown cell. He would remain there until assigned a regular cell.

At 5:00 p.m., they let Father Joe out of his lockdown cell to eat dinner. Walking down a long gray hallway, he entered the dining room. Hundreds of men — all dressed identically — laughed, talked, and ate. Everything was gray. The skin of the men was a sickly gray. Their clothes were dingy. Their voices were a harsh, darker shade of gray. Even the smell of the food was gray, a rancid odor.

As he got in a line and picked up a plastic tray, Father Joe felt depressed. It wasn't his usual depression of deep sadness, loneliness, and lethargy. This new depression hammered him in multiple and unforeseen ways like a machine stamping out brass cymbals. First flattened and left vibrating, then baked.

This wasn't purgatory; this was hell.

Four days later Father Joe did what his attorney had told him to do. He applied to the Intensive Supervision Program. It was for non-violent offenders, a way to ease overcrowding in the prison system. Hugely successful, the program not only saved money but also rehabilitated people. Only 8% of those who entered the program ever went back to crime, whereas 47% of those not in the program soon went back to crime after they were released from prison.

A short time later, Father Joe was accepted into the program despite the objections of the Monmouth County Prosecutor's Office. The prosecutors wanted him to remain in hell for as long as possible. But the prison was self-ruling. It did as it pleased, and it pleased prison officials to run their intensive program.

So, on December 6, 2006, after six months in the confines of prison, Father Joe walked out of prison. To stay out, he had to follow the rules: find a job and work full time, meet twenty times a month with a probation officer, perform sixteen hours of community service each month, and obey a curfew for the next five years. He also had to participate in drug and alcohol testing two times per week. Just one violation of any of the rules and he would go back to hell.

Father Joe moved back into the retreat house at Long Branch. He had nowhere else to go. No one to turn to —

except the Roman Catholic Church. He had no job, no house, no car, and no money.

Reporters contacted the Diocese of Trenton. They wanted to know where Father Joe was. What was his status? Would he do an interview?

A diocesan spokeswoman answered their questions. Her name was Rayanne Bennett. She wasn't a nun. She was a professional specializing in public relations. Young and pretty, she knew how to handle herself. Rayanne declined to reveal Father Hughes' whereabouts. All she said was that "Father Hughes is staying — temporarily — in a retreat house run by a religious order. The retreat house is within the jurisdiction of the diocese."

"What is the name of the retreat house?" asked a reporter who believed in being relentless. If he asked the same question in enough different ways, sometimes he would get an answer.

"I cannot disclose that information," said Rayanne with a smile. She knew all the tricks reporters used.

"How long will Father Hughes stay at the retreat house?" said a reporter.

"Again," said Rayanne, "I cannot say. However, I will tell you that the diocese is providing Father Hughes with a modest stipend. And will continue to do so after he leaves the retreat house."

"Does that mean he's still a priest?"

"Father Hughes remains a priest," said Rayanne. "However, he is on suspension, which means he cannot identify himself as a priest, wear a collar, or celebrate mass."

"Will he be defrocked?" asked a reporter who thought "defrocked" meant being kicked out of the Church.

Rayanne smiled and said sweetly, "'Suspension' is the

preferred term. The Church does not defrock its priests. Once a priest always a priest. The only way to be kicked out of the Church is to be excommunicated. Father Hughes will not be excommunicated."

"Does the diocese have any misgivings about housing and paying a man who stole from the Church?"

"None," said Rayanne. "We have to underscore that Father Hughes remains a diocesan priest, and some provision needs to be made for his basic essentials."

The Diocese of Trenton did not try to distance itself from Father Hughes. In fact, the diocese practiced what it preached — forgiveness and tolerance.

A reporter asked Maureen Oberdorf, a Holy Cross parishioner, how she felt about Father Hughes' release from prison. She said, "I'm happy he's out."

So was Father Joe.

Somewhere near Rumson, New Jersey, Father Joe does daily penance for his sins. He's sixty-four now. His health problems remain. There's no more BMW, no more fancy vacations, no more five-star restaurants.

# CHAPTER 5

# LIVING A LIFE OF LUXURY

THE STORY BEGAN IN PACIFIC PALISADES, New Jersey. Pacific Palisades was a small, blue-collar town. Its inhabitants had large families, worked hard, and attended church on Sundays. The churches boasted youth groups, which catered to young people, who, according to the experts, were "the future of America."

One of those young people was Martin Fay. He played football for St. Cecilia High School. In fact, Martin was co-captain of the team. One of the coaches of the team was named Vince Lombardi.

After graduating from high school, Martin went to war. Joining the U.S. Marine Corps, he fought in the Second World War. When the war was over, he played semi-pro football until he suffered an injury that ended his hope of anything more. So he joined the Pacific Palisades Park police force. Eventually, he became chief of police.

Martin passed away in 1998. He had been honest and

diligent his whole life, and his funeral was well attended. Most of the people recalled, as they listened to the priest, how moral and patient Martin had been.

His name lived on through his five children, whom he and his wife raised to be staunch, God-fearing Catholics. Michael James Fay was the third of the five children.

As Frank Patti, the town mortician, said, "Fay comes from good stock." Patti's hobby was history. Putting his job and his hobby together, he functioned as the unofficial town historian. He buried his parishioners, then wrote about them.

Fay attended parochial schools, where he participated in Catholic youth organizations. He took part in school plays. Being a natural showman, he had a knack for acting and directing.

When he finished high school, Michael decided to go to college. He went to St. Francis University in Loretto, Pennsylvania. But he didn't finish because somewhere in there Michael heard the voice of God. Michael had a calling.

So he moved on to St. Mary's Seminary in Baltimore, where he studied sacred theology. He was preparing for the priesthood. Michael graduated from St. Mary's Seminary in 1977. The first thing he did was change his middle name from James to Jude, after the New Testament apostle. He, too, planned to dedicate his life to God and the Holy Mother Church.

James — the middle name his parents had given him — was biblical too. James was the half-brother of Jesus — for goodness sake — but Jude was better. The name Jude sounded like thunder in Michael Fay's soul, as if God was speaking to Michael from his throne room in heaven.

Michael took Holy Orders in 1978. The princes of the Church sent him to Connecticut, where he served as vicar to

St. Paul's Church in Greenwich. Then he was sent to St. Aloysius Church in New Canaan. Both churches served wealthy parishes. And Michael flourished, being charming, well spoken, and easy to get along with. His supreme talent was fundraising, which made him worth his weight in gold. He would go far in the Church.

In 1991, the powers that be appointed Fay pastor of St. John's Church, the oldest and wealthiest church in Darien. Darien was a small community of 20,000 souls located on what was called Connecticut's "Gold Coast." The term referred to the money found there among many rich, educated people, all of whom had good jobs that they commuted to in the big cities. Ninety percent of Darienites were white, and fully 80% of those were under the age of sixty-five. So Darien was a vibrant place where youth reigned. Money ruled, too, since the average income was $146,755.

All of which made Darien one of the best places to live in America, according to CNN. The price of the average house was $1 million, which meant there was nothing average about Darien. In reality, it was an elite area populated by elite people.

Father Michael Jude Fay was one of them. As the pastor of St. John's, he exhorted his parishioners to have compassion on the poor. St. John's had 1,600 families who heard and responded. Money flowed in. They gave to the tune of $10,000 per week, and that was just the regular collections. All together, the church took in more than $1 million per year.

Father Fay became a guiding star. Everyone loved him. They started calling him Father Jude. His namesake, the Apostle Jude, would have been proud.

The Diocese of Bridgeport loved him, too, since it shared in the wealth. Priests who could raise funds were special.

They had preferred status. As long as the money flowed in, they could pretty much do as they pleased. No one interfered with them.

Sacred Heart University honored Father Jude. It gave him its award for outstanding community service. "Community service" was code for raising a bunch of money. The award meant that Father Jude was the best fundraiser that year. It was a big deal, making the front pages of all the newspapers.

The Bridgeport diocese rewarded him too. It appointed him to the Sexual Misconduct Review Board. Which meant he was somebody.

Only one thing was wrong. Father Jude was dishonest. He should have changed his middle name to Judas rather than Jude. Like Judas, he was willing to sell out Jesus. Unlike Judas, though, Father Jude wanted a lot more than thirty pieces of silver. Father Jude liked the high life, the fast lane, living above the milling throng. But he made only $28,000 per year, along with room and board. Living a life of luxury cost a lot more than that.

St. John's provided Father Jude and his two assistant pastors with credit cards from American Express. The cards were to purchase personal items — within reason — and meals. Since there was no cook provided, the three priests ate all meals at local restaurants. Each month the church would routinely pay off the credit card charges. No one thought anything about it.

Father Jude, being the pastor of the church, was the CFO (chief financial officer) of the church. And the church had plenty of money. So he started spending.

When one of the Sunday School teachers got engaged to be married, Father Jude thought a bridal shower at the church was a good idea. Not only was it a good public relations move, showing how gracious he was, but it was also an opportunity to spend some money. And Father Jude was good at spending money. If possible, he was better at spending money than raising it. He hired a caterer to handle the food and beverages and a three-piece combo to provide the music, and he ordered an extravagant flower arrangement from the local florist.

One day Father Jude noticed how rundown St. John's was looking. Paint was cracking and actually peeling in some spots. And the grounds looked bad. Weeds, no flowers blooming, and the shrubs looked as if they had jaundice or something.

Father Jude made some phone calls. Tradesmen arrived in trucks and vans. A few wanted to submit estimates. Father Jude laughed at the suggestion. He didn't want estimates, which would then be submitted to a committee, which would then argue about the amounts, which would lead to nothing ever getting done. Besides, St. John's Church had no need for committees. The pastor was in charge and living large.

Father Jude hired people on the spot, and work began the next day. Crews of men swarmed over the church building. Carpenters ripped out old pieces of wood, then hammered in new pieces. Painters scraped and sanded and painted. Landscaping crews tore out old plants, dug holes, fertilized, transplanted, replanted. A new sprinkler system was installed — a high-tech one that was programmable.

The rectory where Father Jude and his two assistant pastors lived (in separate apartments) needed to be nicer, which meant, to Father Jude, more luxurious. A good Catholic contractor was hired. He wanted to sign a contract, listing each and every item to be purchased and the work to be performed and the rate of pay and so on.

Father Jude just looked at the guy. "I don't have time for that," he said. "Just send a bill."

The contractor shrugged. It wasn't the way he usually did business. But Father Jude was the priest of a rich mega-church, so he guessed it would be okay. "You got it, Father," he said to the priest. "My guys will be here tomorrow morning bright and early."

"Good," smiled Father Jude, his blue eyes twinkling.

At six o'clock the next morning, all sorts of hammering and pounding and yelling and sawing began. Electricians poked wires here and there. Heavy power cords snaked everywhere. The air filled with sawdust, which puffed up and out and then fell to the ground, where it looked like artificial snow.

All of this, of course, cost thousands of dollars. And no one would or could say anything. Sprucing up the church and expanding the rectory were legitimate expenses.

Once the rectory was finished, Father Jude hired a decorator. New furniture, carpets, appliances — everything was new and top of the line. A beautiful and very expensive tapestry was hung in the common room at the rectory. The moment he saw it in the store, he had to have it. So he bought it. Red and purple and gold, it reminded Father Jude of something King David might have had in the palace in Jerusalem.

After the rectory was finished, several church members took a tour of it. They felt good, for here was proof they took care of their pastors. God would be impressed, they knew, because they were impressed. So God would keep blessing them with more money.

A woman stopped in front of the tapestry. She examined it closely, then turned to Father Jude. "It's beautiful!" she exclaimed. "But the cost must have been prohibitive?"

Father Jude shut her down immediately. "How do you know it wasn't a gift?" he said, then walked away.

The woman bit her lip and flushed.

Father Jude opened a secret bank account in 1999. The name on the account was Bridget Funds. He deposited $230,000 into the account. The money came from St. John's.

Then the heavy spending started. Father Jude bought a new car, an Audi. He went to Cartier and purchased two new Rolexes. Just down the street from the jeweler, he walked into Hermès.

A well-dressed sales associate approached. "May I be of assistance, sir?" he asked. He was surprised by the clergy collar around the man's neck. Not many priests shopped in Hermès. Not many could afford to.

"Certainly," said Father Jude. "I'd like to try on some suits." He glanced around. "The best you have. Maybe something from Italy."

"Of course," said the salesman. He directed the priest to a nearby rack. Plucking at the sleeve of one of the jackets on the rack, the salesman fingered it lightly. Then he leaned forward and sniffed at the material. Looking at the priest, he said, "Armani — the best in the world."

He stepped back so Father Jude could judge for himself. Pretending he knew what he was doing, Father Jude sniffed the material too. The smell of money talked to his nose. He liked it.

An hour later Father Jude walked out of Hermès. There was a spring in his step. He felt important, which ignited a glow of satisfaction in his chest. There was nothing as invigorating as rewarding yourself, he decided.

Five Armani suits at a cost of $15,000 would be ready in

a week. Each would be custom tailored to enhance his tall frame. He'd also dropped a couple of thousand dollars on accessories. Ties, a few shirts, and some socks.

After a few months, the Audi bored Father Jude. It wasn't quite dashing enough. He wanted something lower, longer, and leaner. He paid cash for a new Jaguar XK.

Meanwhile, the Bridget Funds account was running low on money. It needed a transfusion, but Father Jude decided to be careful. So he went to the bank and opened another account, this one under the name of Dombasco. He transferred $750,000 into this account. As before, the money came from St. John's.

Father Jude had a friend named Cliff Fantini. Cliff lived in Philadelphia and ran a wedding-planning business. He consulted on upscale weddings, providing advice on everything from cakes to wedding gowns. Cliff didn't just consult, he functioned as a middleman too. He arranged everything for the bride-to-be. All the bride had to do was tell him what she wanted. Cliff got it, then sent an invoice. Long ago Cliff had decided that Fantini sounded "too Italian," so he had taken Martell as his professional name.

Cliff and Father Jude liked the social scene in Philadelphia. It was far enough away from Darien that Father Jude didn't have to worry about running into anyone he knew. Which meant he could dispose of his clergy collar and act like a normal human being. Which meant he could wear his new Armani suits. Tall and handsome, he looked a lot like Ray Milland of movie fame.

Eventually, the two men decided to buy a condo in Philadelphia. That way Cliff could move out of his apartment, which was getting crowded because he ran his business out of it. They put $39,558 down on the condo, $34,000 of which came from St. John's Church. It was easy. Father Jude told one of his office workers at the church to transfer $34,000 from a parish bank account in Connecticut to his personal bank account at Wachovia Bank in Florida. Then he simply transferred the funds from Florida to Philadelphia. The $34,000 was money that was supposed to be used to pay day-to-day parish expenses and church employees.

Father Jude had a bank account in Florida because he and Cliff were planning to buy another condo down there. They had one all picked out; it cost only $495,000. Father Jude simply transferred more money from St. John's into his account.

Cliff and Father Jude liked to go shopping. They would hire a limo, which would drive them into the big city. Father Jude bought Cliff some jewelry at Tiffany's in New York. While there, they ate at the Manhattan Grille; when that got boring, they ate at the Willett House over in tony Port Chester. Father Jude and Cliff enjoyed being around other people of quality and means. Sometimes, just for a change, they took a limo over to the Homestead Inn in Greenwich.

In Philadelphia, they were regular customers at Bookbinder's restaurant, the most expensive in the city. And each month they spent hours selecting hundreds of dollars worth of wine. Some they took back to their condo, the rest they had shipped back to Darien.

One day at the condo in Philadelphia, Cliff said, "Jude, I really wish I could do more advertising for my business. But it's so darn expensive."

"Why do you need to advertise?" asked Father Jude. "I thought your business was doing well."

"It is," admitted Cliff. "But with weddings you never know when things might slack off. People need to know I'm here."

"Okay," said Father Jude. "Have some ads put together. Tell them to send me the bill."

"Really?" said Cliff, excited.

"Sure."

A while later *Philadelphia Style* magazine sent an invoice for $10,000. Cliff had placed some full-page ads in the magazine. Father Jude paid it without comment. It was a drop in the bucket.

*Philadelphia Style* magazine was a slick publication that catered to well-heeled snobs in the city. Occasionally, the magazine devoted itself to what it called "a theme issue." In the January-February issue that year, wedding planner Clifford Martell was featured in a lengthy article with other couples, all of whom were beautiful, successful, and hip. Cliff and Jude were one of the couples interviewed. The issue was billed as "the sexiest issue ever" and asked the question, "Where was your most romantic Philadelphia dining experience?" Cliff and Jude answered, "La Boheme because it's intimate with delicious food."

The article went on to describe their luxury condo in Philadelphia, their luxury apartment on Manhattan's East 63rd Street, and their "get-away" luxury condo in Fort Lauderdale. There was a photo of them: Cliff with his arms wrapped around Jude's shoulders. Jude wore a three-piece Armani suit with a purple tie, while Cliff was in black, French cuffs, and diamond cufflinks. The photo had been taken at another "swells event" — the Alliance for Philadelphia's Animals annual fundraiser. Father Jude was identified simply as Michael Jude Fay, and neither the article nor the caption under the photo mentioned he was a priest in the Catholic Church. Probably because Father Jude had never mentioned it either.

The same issue of the magazine carried a full-page ad for Martell's wedding-planning business.

A few years earlier, in 2001, Father Jude had been diagnosed with prostate cancer. His doctor assured him they had caught it in time. A short course of chemotherapy should take care of it. No big deal. No worries, as they said in Philadelphia.

Father Jude made sure everyone at St. John's and the Bridgeport diocese knew about his cancer. It was a good excuse to be away from the church, which was really getting boring. He called it "his cancer card." Whenever he wanted to get out of town or didn't want to do something — such as talk to parishioners or give counseling or listen to confessions — he played his cancer card. He assigned his assistant pastor, Father Madden, to do all the boring chores. Father Madden was forty-something, good looking, energetic, and dedicated. He had a nice bedside manner that the parishioners especially liked.

Most months Father Jude wasn't around much. He'd spend a week or two at the church, then take off on vacation. He and Cliff would fly down to Florida or take a cruise or fly to Europe, where they enjoyed local cuisine and went sightseeing. Of course, Father Jude told the church that he was going to New York for more cancer treatments. What the parishioners didn't know wouldn't hurt them, he decided.

When Father Jude was at the church, Cliff was usually there too. Cliff had a knack for getting in the way.

One day Ellen Patafio cornered Father Madden. Ellen was the church secretary. "That man," she whispered to

Father Madden, "is turning this place upside down. He seems to think we work for him. If I'm in the middle of a conversation on the phone, he comes into the office and interrupts me to say, 'I need tape, I need that.' He even tells people to get up from the computer so he can use it." She paused to glance over at Cliff, who was on the other side of the office using the copy machine. "He has no regard for us conducting business," she said in a spitting whisper.

Father Madden nodded. "I know how you feel," he said. "I'll see what I can do about it. Maybe have a private word with Father Jude."

"Well, something needs to be done," said Ellen. "And I don't think talking to Father Jude is going to do anything. He and Father Jude sit down and start telling their stories." She stared at Father Madden to see if he knew what kind of stories she was referring to.

Father Madden nodded. He knew.

"It's inappropriate," seethed Ellen. "I'll tell you the truth, Father. I don't feel comfortable when that man is here."

"I know, Ellen," said Father Madden. "I'm concerned too. Very concerned." He raised his eyebrows. "I'll see what I can do."

On the weekends that Father Jude remained at the church, especially when Cliff was there, they would have parties in the rectory. Lots of booze, lots of good food prepared by a chef, and sometimes live music. The place really jumped. It was great fun. It was also a touch too much.

Frank Colandro, who owned Mama Carmela's Deli across from St. John's Church, saw Cliff Martell walking his frou-frou dog on the church grounds. "I asked the people who worked there when I first saw this guy," said Colandro. "They said it's his boyfriend." Colandro said it was wrong. A priest openly conducting a romantic relationship. "You're slapping the parishioners in the face when you do that, when you're flaunting your boyfriend around," he said.

It was April 2006 when things began to crumble.

Father Madden had been going through hell for the last four years. Father Jude was forsaking his holy vows as a priest. That was obvious. And, what was worse, Father Madden suspected Father Jude of being a thief.

Father Madden got sick to his stomach at every Sunday mass. He'd look out at all those parishioners — people who had faith in God and the Church — and he'd know they were being hoodwinked. Father Jude was duping them. And he felt guilty because he didn't say anything. He didn't know what to do, so he prayed about it. God answered his prayer.

Bethany Derario was the bookkeeper for St. John's Church. But she couldn't do her job because Father Jude wouldn't provide credit card receipts. The priest was spending money like crazy. She didn't know how much because there was no accounting going on. She didn't even know how much money the church really had anymore. One more time she confronted him. "Father Jude," she said, "please, I need you to give me your credit card statements."

"I'll get you what you need," said Father Jude, stalling. He went back to his office and found some stubs from American Express. All they showed was the total spent. Nothing was itemized.

The next morning he left them on the bookkeeper's desk.

Three hours later Bethany knocked on Father Jude's office door.

"Come in," he said.

Bethany walked in, holding the stubs in her hand.

"Oh, Bethany," said Father Jude. He sounded disappointed and irritated.

"Father Jude," she said, "I have to have itemized receipts. Payment stubs won't do." She held up the worthless pieces of paper he had dumped on her desk.

Father Jude was frustrated and angry. Why was this woman always hounding him? He was the pastor of St. John's. The priestly entitlements belonged to him. No one had the right to question his authority. Especially some female bookkeeper. Didn't she know who he was? Enough was enough. Holier-than-thou fury bloated him. "You'll never get the Amex," he raged, his face purple with passion. "It's none of your business what I spend the money on."

Bethany fled the office and went back to her desk. Holding back tears, she started to sit down, then she changed her mind and walked out. She went looking for Father Madden.

When she told Father Madden what had happened, he nodded slowly. "Bethany," he said, "I've suspected wrongdoing for a long time. I think it's time we did something. Gather everything you've got and meet me outside. We're going to Bridgeport."

"Okay," said Bethany.

On the afternoon of April 28, 2006, Bethany Derario and Father Madden drove to Bridgeport. Sitting on the back seat of the car was a box full of financial records, all from St. John's Church. The Archdiocese of Bridgeport had its offices in an old, ugly building that looked more like a union hall in Milwaukee than the blessed command center of the Holy Mother Church. At the archdiocese, they met with Norm Walker. Norm was the chief financial officer of the diocese. Amy Hermanns, one of Walker's staff accountants, sat in on the meeting.

Walker came right to the point. He was a busy man and didn't have time for games. "What's the problem?" he asked.

"The problem is we don't know how much money St. John's has," said Father Madden. "Or exactly how much is being spent. But we do know that Father Jude is spending money like crazy."

"I don't understand," said Walker, rubbing his chin. "St. John's is a wealthy church. Money comes in, and money goes out." He looked at Bethany. "The bookkeeper keeps track."

"Not if receipts are not produced," said Father Madden as he shifted uncomfortably in his chair. He felt like Judas. "Look," he said, "Father Jude is spending tremendous amounts of money on extravagances."

"Like what?" said Walker.

"Parties, vacations, eating out, and other things we can't keep track of."

Walker exchanged glances with Hermann. "Okay," said Walker. "It sounds serious. In fact, I am now concerned." He leaned forward. "Leave your records, and we'll go over them. Then I'll report to the bishop and let you know what we find."

As Father Madden and Bethany Derario walked out to their car, Bethany said, "Finally."

Father Madden nodded. "I think they're going to do something about it," he said.

"Me, too," agreed Bethany.

A few days later Bishop Lori ordered Father Jude to Bridgeport. The financial team of Walker and Hermanns had sat down with the bishop. They told him that the bookkeeping at St. John's Church was a disaster. A lot of money was being spent, but it probably looked worse than it really was. They didn't think there was any funny business going on. In fact, there was no evidence of anything but mismanagement. Walker and Hermanns seemed more concerned with Bethany Derario. Hermanns suggested that perhaps it was time for St. John's to get a new bookkeeper.

After hearing their report, Bishop Lori relaxed. The potential for crisis had passed. It was just mismanagement of funds, common throughout the Catholic Church. Which was understandable because priests didn't hold MBAs from the Wharton School of Business. Trained in theology and spiritual counseling, they had neither the time nor the inclination to balance spreadsheets. What's more, Father Jude was the single best fundraiser in the diocese. Bishop Lori did not expect the man to bring it in and then count it too. Professionals could do that. And Father Jude had other things on his mind. Such as cancer. That would upset anyone and certainly explain any accounting hodgepodge.

Bishop Lori had summoned Father Jude to the meeting so he could gently and tactfully suggest that Father Jude provide a little more financial oversight. Like Hermanns suggested — maybe a new bookkeeper. Or perhaps an assistant, some layman who could handle the tedious details for Father Jude. That way he could continue to raise funds and not get bogged down in nonsense.

In response to the ecclesiastical summons, Father Jude boarded a plane in Ft. Lauderdale, where he was vacationing at his luxury waterfront condo. He loved the beaches of white sand. And the nightlife in Ft. Lauderdale was brilliant. Lots of nightclubs, neon lights, showy clothing, and great performances. All the people played a part, pretending they were someone else, leaving their real selves behind. It was like a giant melodrama.

His plane landed in New York City on May 8th. Father

Jude took a suite at the Ritz-Carlton for the night. On May 9th, he drove to Bridgeport for his meeting with Bishop Lori.

No one really knows what took place at the meeting or who said what. None of the attendees would talk about it. Present were Bishop Lori, Norm Walker, and Monsignor Peter Cullen, vicar general of the diocese. Which meant he was the assistant bishop.

Whatever happened in the meeting, when it was over Father Jude still had his job, still lived in the rectory, and was still pastor of St. John's Church. After he left the meeting, he went straight to the airport and got on a plane — back to Ft. Lauderdale.

Back in Darien, at St. John's Church, Bethany Derario heard about what had occurred at the meeting in Bridgeport. Father Madden told her. She couldn't believe it. "You mean nothing happened?"

"Nothing," said Father Madden. "Somehow he talked his way out of it."

"That's not right!" exclaimed Bethany.

Father Madden shrugged. "I know. But that's their decision. He remains pastor of St. John's."

"We have to do something," said Bethany, urgency in her voice. "He can't keep doing this."

"I have an idea," said Father Madden, lowering his voice. "We hire a private investigator. Tell him what we know and what we suspect. Then ask him to get proof."

Bethany looked at him with wide eyes. "Do we dare do that?" she whispered.

"We have no choice. Not if we want to put a stop to this," said Father Madden.

Bethany thought about it for a moment. "Okay," she said.

"Let's do it."

The next day they drove to the Stamford, Connecticut, office of private investigator Vito Colucci. Once again, in the car with them, on the back seat, were copies of St. John's financial records. Colucci took the job. Father Madden and Bethany Derario paid his retainer fee with their own money.

After a one-week investigation, Vito Colucci and his associate Wendy Kleinknecht discovered that Father Jude had spent $200,000 in the month of May alone. Most of the money had gone to wine and dine Cliff Martell.

Colucci called Father Madden and told him what they had found. "I only went back two years," said Colucci. "So it's worse than it looks. The guy has been stealing money for years."

"What do we do now?" asked Father Madden.

"Legally, I have to report this — a felony — to the police," said Colucci.

"When?"

"Right now," said Colucci.

Half an hour later Colucci and Kleinknecht walked into the Darien Police Station carrying a box of evidence. They sat down with police investigators. One hour later the Darien Police placed a call to Bishop Lori in Bridgeport. Ten minutes after that call, Bishop Lori called Father Jude on his private cell phone. Apart from the bishop and Father Jude, no one knew what was said. But when he hung up, Father Michael Jude Fay was no longer the pastor of St. John's Church. On May 17, 2006, he resigned.

The Associated Press immediately picked up on the story. Unholy and sensational, it was just the kind of thing the media love.

The reports said that Fay had resigned after the diocese had learned that some of the church's bills hadn't been paid and that there appeared to be other financial problems. This was according to the diocesan spokesman, Joseph McAleer. He went on to say that Fay was cooperating with the investigation. Note, too, that Father Jude was now referred to simply as Fay. Everyone was trying to distance him from the Church.

Vito Colucci told reporters that he was responsible for the priest's resignation and the investigation. He said he had documentation that at least $200,000 of parish funds had been spent on trips, dinners at gourmet restaurants, and limousines.

When asked about Colucci and his proof, McAleer didn't know what to say. "The diocese did not hire Mr. Colucci," said McAleer. "And cannot deny or confirm his findings. Fay's resignation was based on the church's own investigation into church finances and Fay's personal suitability for the priesthood. This investigation has been ongoing for some time."

"Who hired you?" a reporter asked Colucci.

"I can't say," said Colucci. "Except to say they are connected to the church."

Needless to say, the members of St. John's Church were bewildered.

Kris Wray admitted to being shocked. "It was very surprising," she said. "I think a lot of us knew that Father Jude was not acting like he had acted years ago. We assumed he was absent because of his cancer treatments. We've always liked his pastoral care when he was there to give it. I have asked him for things, and he's always been fantastic. It's just lately he hasn't been there for us as we would have liked."

Another woman said, "Everybody was wondering what was going on. But no one would have noticed anything amiss with church finances. Because it's a large church and very wealthy."

Veronica Sedita said, "Everything seemed to be in tip-top shape. It certainly comes as a shock because I thought everything was going smoothly. It doesn't seem like it's possible, but I guess it is."

John Ford said, "From a personal point of view, I respected his position." Ford admitted, though, that he didn't know Fay personally.

On May 22, 2006, Bishop Lori made an appearance at St. John's Church. His black limousine purred up in front of the church. He and his staff emerged from behind the tinted windows.

It was Sunday mass, when most of the active members would be at the church. In fact, this Sunday it was standing room only. Bishop Lori stood before the crowd and apologized. "I am truly sorry for this scandal," he said. "But I promise you that the Bridgeport diocese will investigate and get to the bottom of this. It is precisely in these moments of tension, disappointment, anger, and sadness that the quality and capacity of our love is tested. I am deeply sorry that this parish is going through such a severe test and came in person to apologize."

He went on to tell the congregation that the diocese had hired Deloitte and Touche to conduct a full forensic investigation of the church's books. "A considerable portion of your offerings were used to fund a lifestyle that no follower of Christ, particularly a priest, should lead. The diocese will try to make restitution and will keep the parish council informed of any and all results. Whatever your feelings and mine may be, we also need to pray for Father Fay and everyone else involved in this crisis," said the bishop.

He then instructed his staff to distribute copies of a letter he had written to the congregation.

After the mass, as they filed slowly out, everyone came face to face with television crews, newspaper reporters, and photographers. There was no avoiding them, for scandal sold well.

Norm Walker, the chief financial officer of the diocese, stopped in front of the television crews and was asked by a reporter about the private investigator. "We still don't know who hired the private investigator," Walker said. "However, the diocese had already begun looking into the matter last year."

"How much money was stolen?" asked the reporter, referring to the $200,000 figure.

"I can neither deny nor confirm the $200,000 figure," said Walker. "We don't know if that is accurate or not because the investigation is in its infancy. However, I can tell you that suspicions surfaced at the diocese last year when we noted expenses for St. John's, such as food and travel, had increased as much as 150% compared to the previous year."

"What did you do about it?" asked the reporter. "What action did you take?"

"We immediately began our own investigation," said Walker. "There were delinquent payments to some employee benefit plans. And earlier this year People's Bank notified the diocese that a loan was overdue."

Bishop Lori stood next to Norm Walker. He approved of Norm's statements by nodding in a grim manner. Then the bishop said, "I have known Father Fay for five years, and I have visited St. John's Church many times. My hope is that the investigation will determine exactly what happened. And I hope the church remains united. I know it's a great and strong community."

Nancy Matthews, chief legal counsel for the diocese and a tall, striking woman, stood next to Bishop Lori. "We never knew anything about this," said Matthews.

"What happens now?" asked a television reporter.

"While the investigation continues, I have appointed Father Michael Madden as acting administrator of St. John's," said Bishop Lori. "I will appoint a permanent administrator as soon as possible. Also, I and my staff plan on attending every mass at St. John's this weekend."

The reporters pressed in with more questions, but Bishop Lori and Norm Walker said they had said enough for now. They walked to the waiting limousine, got in, and left.

Looking for new offerings to stoke the fires of sensationalism, the cameras stalked members of the congregation. A few stopped and spoke.

"Father Fay is a human being like everyone else," said Martha Gelineau. "I pray for him. He is a great man."

Seventy-six-year-old Rose Bivona locked horns with the cameras without fear. At her age, not much bothered her. "Father Jude is very, very special. I'm not saying he was God, but he really had something special about him," Rose said. "I think that parishioners of this church are very strong people. They'll spring back quickly. I don't think there's been any anger, just disappointment and sadness."

Instead of getting better, things got worse.

That same day Father Michael Madden resigned. More than likely, he had been told to resign by Bishop Lori. In other words, he had been fired but given the opportunity to save his pride by resigning. The story that he voluntarily resigned was a smokescreen, a little fib that the diocese came up with.

That day — in the early morning hours — Father Madden told the congregation he was resigning. He admitted that he and Bethany Derario had hired the private investigator who had brought down Father Jude. They had paid the investigator — Vito Colucci — with their own money. The bishop had found out just the day before.

"I'm sorry Father Jude did what he did," said Madden. "I'm sorry that the accountant and the finance board were asleep at the switch. And I am sorry and angry that the diocese failed to come to my rescue when there were red flags waving everywhere." Dressed in his vestments, Father Madden stood behind his pulpit. "The past four years have been a living hell for me. Right now the diocese is ripping mad at me and Bethany for what we saw as a prudent effort to protect ourselves. I don't know what is going to happen to me now, but whatever it is it will be a welcome relief from the extreme physical and emotional strain I have been suffering. I simply could not stand behind that altar and look out at you good people knowing what was being done to you."

Father Madden told it like it was. Sounding more like a hell-fire-and-damnation Baptist preacher, he had just blasted the church's finance committee, the church accountant, and the Bridgeport diocese. In the bishop's eyes, Father Madden had gone renegade by hiring a private investigator. In simple terms, he was a traitor, possibly an apostate.

Such a rebellious move also suggested that the bishop had blundered in his duties. So Bishop Lori probably reprimanded Father Madden and demanded his resignation. This was obvious from Father Madden's remarks to his parishioners: the diocese was "ripping mad" at him, and he didn't know what was going to happen to him now.

Later that afternoon the diocese released a letter to the parishioners of St. John's Church. The letter was from Father Madden. But it was clear from the way Father Madden did an about-face from his angry remarks of that morning that he had been told to get back in line. Stop rocking the boat.

In the letter, Father Madden apologized. "At mass this morning, and in conversations with many of you, I spoke way out of turn and suggested things regarding Bishop William Lori and the Diocese of Bridgeport which were not true or factual, in reference to the investigation of Father Fay's financial stewardship of our parish," he wrote.

In addition, Father Madden took the blame. It was his fault. He shouldn't have done what he did. To that end, he wrote, "The Diocese had no knowledge that I hired an investigator. In hindsight, I realize I made a huge mistake, which has further complicated matters. In my actions and words, I betrayed your trust and the trust of my bishop, who has been working diligently to deal with the situation at hand and to arrive at the truth of these matters. I also misled you into doubting that the diocese is fully engaged in vigorously working for a just and prudent resolution of this matter."

Reactions to the letter were hostile. Everybody knew what had taken place. Father Madden had been told to sit down and shut up, to stop telling the truth and start playing Church politics.

Michael Sherman said, "Nothing was being done about it. It didn't look like anything was going to be done about it, so they kind of went outside the chain of command, hired a private investigator, and told him to look into this and deliver his findings to the appropriate law enforcement authorities."

Sherman was Bethany Derario's attorney. Bethany had seen how things were going, so she had hired an attorney to protect herself. Sherman was asked why Bethany had hired him. "She may not need an attorney. She is not being accused of any wrongdoing, and I do not expect that she will. We have no lawsuits that we're working up. But it's a scary situation where you are dealing with law enforcement authorities from many places, and she needs some guidance."

A member of St. John's Church, eighty-one-year-old Veronica Sedita said, "Oh, my God. I don't know what to think of anything anymore. Everything seemed so nice and happy, well run on the surface."

Bishop Lori said, "I am deeply saddened by the latest developments. They have cast a shadow on all the hard work the diocese has done to be open and honest with the parish family of St. John's about this extremely difficult situation." The bishop went on to say that he had appointed Father William J. Scheyd to take over as pastor of St. John's Parish. Father Madden would remain as an assistant.

Later that same chaotic day in May, Bishop Lori and his staff once again arrived at St. John's to meet with the Parish Council and the Finance Committee. By now it was six o'clock in the evening. Father Madden was there too. He had been ordered to attend the meeting. His presence was supposed to ease any doubts the committee members might have.

Word of the meeting got around, and many parishioners showed up at the church. They resembled an angry mob, like the farmers and peasants converging on Dr. Frankenstein's castle. The parishioners told Bishop Lori that Father Madden had acted out of love and should not be spanked for blowing the whistle.

Stunned by the righteous wrath of the 200 church members, Bishop Lori defended himself. "I do not think it was the right thing to bring this thing to a private investigator, who unceremoniously brought it to the media before we had a chance to investigate," said the bishop, who wore the full regalia of his office. "We are not a corporation, we are not a government agency, we are a church community, and it's best we come together to decide how to handle the difficulties."

Someone shouted, "Why didn't you get rid of Father Jude when you knew there were problems with the church's finances?"

"We do not ask a pastor to step aside when we audit his parish," said Bishop Lori, who looked as if he had just been slapped. "When we began, we had no reason to believe there was wrongdoing. We thought perhaps there was mismanagement. When we realized something was wrong, I asked Father Fay to resign."

"When did you learn that Father Jude was stealing from his church?" demanded a voice from the crowd.

"Sometime this spring," said the bishop.

"That's awfully vague," shouted a man. "Just exactly when?"

The bishop shilly-shallied. There were more insistent questions that the bishop tried to answer. His replies only stirred the crowd up more.

Father Madden stood up from his seat by the altar. He tried to calm everyone down. "I apologize — again — for complicating this," he said. "Please calm down. The bishop deserves our respect. It's not his fault that Father Jude did what he did." Father Madden looked over at Bishop Lori. "He's been very kind to me in light of my transgressions," said the priest.

Boos erupted from the crowd. "He covered it up," shouted a woman's voice.

Father Madden held up his hands, pleading for quiet. "I don't want to be the pastor at this time," he said, raising his voice over the hullabaloo. "Even if Bishop Lori offered me the job as pastor, I don't feel quite ready to assume that. I'm busy enough as an associate here."

His words didn't work. Angry as hornets, the crowd hissed and demanded answers.

Finally, Bishop Lori held up his hands. The room got quiet. "I will report back to you when our investigation is completed." Then he walked away with his staff in tow.

Dissatisfied, the congregation remained behind, talking among themselves. Then they spoke to the media, who had gathered outside the church. Most insisted that Father Madden had no reason to apologize. A number of them said they did not believe Father Madden had written the letter the diocese had distributed. Others wanted to talk about Father Jude.

"We should be thanking him for bringing this to our attention," said one man, speaking of Father Madden.

Phillip Dolcetti told a reporter, "We feel that Father Mike [Madden] is going to be here temporarily, and then they are going to put him out to pasture."

Julie Rikert said, "I don't think they were treating the bishop well for his position. They didn't show any respect when these men got up and shouted. I just had my hands up and was praying because I thought there was going to be a riot." Referring to Father Jude, she added, "We knew his lifestyle. We wondered where the money went. I think part of it is our fault. We weren't involved enough."

Ed Sforza, president of the Parish Council, said,

"Parishioners did question me about his extravagance, and I did question Father Jude. His answer was 'Oh, I think I have good taste, and I do things in a tasteful manner.'"

"He was living the high life and stealing from the parish," said Phillip Dolcetti.

Father Michael Jude Fay had still not been formally charged with any crime. Yet his legal costs kept piling up. He had no money to pay his attorney's fees. His source of money had been St. John's Church, an Old Faithful supply of cash that was now as dry as the Sahara Desert. His sense of entitlement, however, had not dried up.

So Father Jude sent out a letter describing his monetary woes to many of his former parishioners. The letter ended with this plea for money: "As you can only imagine, this past year has been complicated and extremely painful. As proceedings come to a conclusion, I am left with a very difficult legal bill — $115,000. I am reaching out to my family and friends for help. Contributions may be addressed to the Hartford law firm, Robinson & Cole, which is representing me."

Bill Rowe, a deacon at St. John's, summed up everyone's opinion of the letter. "You'd think he would ask for forgiveness and then ask for some money," Rowe said. "But to come out and say help me out, he's depending on us. I'm pretty sure he's got plenty of money stashed away somewhere."

On June 4, 2006, Joseph McAleer made a statement to the press. McAleer enjoyed being the diocesan spokesman. He got to custom-build announcements for just the right effect. "The Rev. Frank McGrath will begin his new appointment at St. John's Church tomorrow," said McAleer. "Rev. McGrath is the director of clergy personnel for the Diocese of Bridgeport and is one of Bishop Lori's closest advisers. St. John's in Darien is a parish that has really been crying out for good news, and that's what was given."

McAleer then read from a written statement by Bishop Lori praising Reverend McGrath. "He has extensive and invaluable experience as a pastor, and connects easily and warmly with all age groups. I am confident that the parish family of St. John's in Darien will grow to love and respect Father McGrath as a spiritual leader and a friend. I have the utmost faith in him."

McAleer then added, "Father Madden and Father Bill Platt will remain as associate pastors."

Bishop Lori was sending in his best closer. Father McGrath was a fixer. When the diocese found itself in a jam, it called on Father McGrath. He had taken over another church in the diocese in 2002 when the pastor of that church had been charged with sex abuse. Father McGrath had come in and waved his magic wand of healing and reconciliation.

Clearly, his appointment to St. John's meant the church was sinking fast.

The scandal just wouldn't go away. In fact, it got worse and worse.

In July 2006, Father Jude's relationship with Cliff Fantini became hot news. No one used the words *gay relationship*, but everyone knew that's what was meant.

Through his spokesman, Joseph McAleer, Bishop Lori made it crystal clear that he had no knowledge of Father Fay's sexuality. "The bishop had met with Father Fay many times in his time as pastor but was not aware of his apparent relationship," said McAleer. He then went on to say that Bishop Lori had asked for Father Fay's resignation as soon as he heard of the relationship with Cliff Fantini/Martell. "The priesthood is a higher calling, so a priest is required, at a minimum, to lead a moral life and follow the teachings of the Church," McAleer said. "Clearly, that wasn't the case with Father Fay."

A reporter asked, "Where is Father Fay now?"

McAleer said, "The diocese is not aware of his whereabouts. All communication with Father Fay is through his attorney."

"Is he still employed by the diocese?" asked another reporter.

"Father Fay cannot and does not function as a priest," said McAleer. "However, he does receive a modest stipend from the diocese for his living expenses."

Ellen Patafio was the secretary at St. John's when Father Jude was the pastor. She came out and said what most wanted to say but didn't. "Cliff was his life. He would do anything for Cliff."

Leo Mocato disagreed with anyone who called Father Jude a homosexual. Leo was a chef who had been employed as a caterer by Father Jude. Leo said there was nothing inappropriate about the two men's relationship. He had catered most of the rectory parties and was an eyewitness to the festivities. He told reporters what he had seen. "They were good, clean parties with a lot of damn good food and some good wine," he said. "He wasn't hiding anything. There were parishioners there. I think they are trying to make this very sensationalized with the gay lover, which I don't even think is true."

Leo went on to say that Father Jude was a great fundraiser and that was why the church and the diocese loved him. "With his good taste and flair for decorating, he fixed up the whole church. It was a dump until he got there."

Finally, Leo told the reporters what he thought about the diocese and its lavish ways as a whole. "I've cooked for lots of the priests in the diocese," he said. "And they all want nothing but the best. Go audit every priest in the diocese. You'd be shocked where they eat."

In August 2006, Father Michael Jude Fay still had not been charged with any crimes. Fraud, grand theft by embezzlement, and illegal interstate transfer of funds were likely. The interstate transfer of funds offense made it a federal case. So the feds arrived and began their own investigation.

Investigators determined that Father Jude had stolen $1.3 million from St. John's between 2000 and 2006. Some evidence pointed to the figure being as high as $2.5 million.

Lawrence Hopkins was Father Jude's attorney. Hopkins was both smart and experienced with the feds. He was also a realist.

"You have two options," said Hopkins to Father Jude. "Number one is that you plead guilty to a lesser charge. In that scenario, you will receive a short prison sentence."

"How short is short?" asked Father Jude.

"Three to five years," said Hopkins. Considering the circumstances, Hopkins considered three to five years a gift from the gods. "Option number two is we take it to trial." Hopkins put his right hand in his pocket, where he had eighty cents in change. As he looked out the window, he jiggled the pocket, listening to the change jingle. Then he turned to Father Jude and looked him in the eye. "We won't win," he said. "There's a paper trail behind you a mile wide. In this scenario, you go to prison for ten to fifteen years."

"So I'm pretty much fucked is what you're telling me,

right?" said Father Jude, grimacing at his predicament.

"Pretty much," said Hopkins.

"But I'm not guilty of anything," said Father Jude. "I had a right to spend money on vacations, airline tickets, housing, and food. I had the right to eat at any restaurant I wanted as frequently as I wanted. I had a right to hire limousine service." The Reverend Michael Jude Fay really believed what he was saying.

"Father," said Hopkins in an exasperated tone, "we've been over this. You may think what you did was acceptable. However, I can assure you that the jury will not."

Father Jude stared off into space.

Jingling the coins in his pocket one more time, Hopkins reached for his briefcase. As he walked toward the door, he said, "I'll make the deal." He closed the door behind him.

Still staring at nothing, Father Jude spoke to the empty room. "I didn't do anything wrong."

One week later, in wealthy Darien, Bethany Derario resigned her position as bookkeeper. When she told Father McGrath she was leaving, he didn't seem surprised.

Later, in private conversation with her attorney, she told him she was being harassed. "Because I blew the whistle on them," she said. "The diocese wants me out."

Her attorney asked her if she wanted to sue the diocese.

"Not right now," she said. "I just need some rest for a while. I can't take any more stress right now."

"Okay," said the attorney. "I understand. If you change your mind, we can work up a lawsuit later."

Three weeks after Bethany Derario quit her job as parish bookkeeper another dramatic event took place. Father

Michael Madden not only resigned from the parish of St. John's but quit the priesthood entirely. Father Madden was forty-five. The priesthood was his life. The Holy Mother Church was his soul.

When he walked into Father McGrath's office to announce his decision, his bags were already packed. Father McGrath tried to talk him out of it. He suggested a leave of absence for a while. Father Madden just shook his head and left.

When the press heard about it, they flocked to St. John's. Father McGrath said, "I know that for years he had inner turmoil over his vocation, and he had some bad experiences over the years, including his relationship with the diocese."

At the Bridgeport diocese, Joseph McAleer said, "How upsetting, confusing, and tragic this is for someone not only to leave their post but announce a treasured vocation has ended. We hope Father Madden will reconsider his decision. If so, the diocese will welcome him back to continue serving as a priest."

No one knew whether Father Madden had been forced out or not.

Vito Colucci, the private investigator hired by Father Madden, had his opinion. "I think he realized that, once the story was out, it was only a matter of time. I think he was the object of retaliation."

When the congregation of St. John's Church was told, many began weeping.

On September 12, 2007, Father Michael Jude Fay stood with his attorney in the courtroom at the New Haven Federal Courthouse. Father Jude wore a black Armani suit, a black tie, and a white shirt. He was fifty-six. His hair had turned white. There was no need for the blond highlights he used to have his hairdresser add.

U.S. District Court Judge Janet Bond Arterton sat on the bench. She asked if Father Fay waived his right to trial.

"We do, Your Honor," said his attorney, Lawrence Hopkins.

Judge Arterton asked if Father Fay understood what that meant.

"He does, Your Honor," said Hopkins. He had already explained to Father Jude that, by pleading guilty, he also waived his right to appeal. Unless, of course, his sentence was more than fifty-seven months. If it was more than fifty-seven months, then they could appeal. That was the deal he had hammered out with the feds.

"Do you wish to plead guilty?" asked the judge.

"Yes, Your Honor," said Father Jude.

"What are you pleading guilty to?" said Judge Arterton.

"I used church funds for means other than the needs of the parish or the parishioners," explained Father Jude.

"Were the funds obtained by theft or by fraud?"

"By fraud," said Father Jude.

"Were the funds transferred through interstate commerce?"

"Yes, Your Honor. Through credit cards and bank accounts."

"Were you fully aware that the funds you were using were gained by fraud?"

"Yes, Your Honor," said Father Jude.

Richard J. Schechter, the federal prosecutor, rose and detailed Father Jude's crimes. The prosecutor enlightened the court about the expensive baubles the priest had purchased. He described the lavish vacations and the luxury condominiums and the $130,000 spent on limousines. All together the amount stolen was $1,014,000.

When the prosecutor finished, Father Jude seemed confused. "May I consult with my attorney?" he asked the judge.

"Certainly," said Arterton.

Father Jude and Hopkins whispered to each other for a few minutes. When they finished, Father Jude faced the judge.

"Your Honor, I do not dispute that I gained the money illicitly. However, I am unsure of the specific numbers that were just related," said Father Jude.

He was concerned about the million-dollar figure because it would determine the length of his sentence. If he stole between $400,000 and $1 million, then his prison sentence would range between thirty-seven and forty-six months. If he stole more than $1 million, then he faced forty-six to fifty-seven months in prison.

The judge nodded to the court clerk. "Duly noted, Father Fay," said the judge. She looked at the attorneys. "Attorneys will satisfy the exact amount."

Hopkins and Schechter nodded.

Judge Arterton set bail at $50,000 and directed Father Jude to surrender his passport immediately. "Your travel will be restricted to Connecticut and Florida, where you will report to probation officers as scheduled. Travel to New York, New Jersey, and Pennsylvania will require prior written notice to probation," said the judge.

Hopkins rose and said, "Your Honor, we respectfully request permission to travel to New York, as Father Fay is undergoing medical treatment there. We also respectfully request permission to travel to New Jersey. That is where Father Fay's mother lives."

"Qualified permission is granted," said the judge. "Prior

written notice being the qualification."

"If there is nothing else," said Arterton, looking at the attorneys — who both shook their heads — "sentencing will take place on December 4, 2007."

For now, it was over. Outside Father Jude had to run the media gauntlet. He refused to make any comment.

Within minutes of Father Jude's plea of guilty, the Bridgeport diocese issued a formal statement.

> The Bridgeport Diocese thanks the FBI and the U.S. Attorney's Office for its comprehensive investigation and efforts to bring this unfortunate issue to conclusion. We pray that today's announcement will help the St. John Parish community put a sad chapter of its history behind it and finalize the healing process that has been so ably overseen by its pastor, Father Frank McGrath.
>
> With Father Fay's plea of guilty on the charges of interstate transportation of funds he obtained by fraud, the diocese has affirmed that he remains unauthorized to function as a priest, as has been the case for more than a year.

Reporters asked Father McGrath for his reaction to the plea. He gave a lengthy formal statement claiming that St. John's was doing better than ever.

Susan Byrne, on the Parish Council of St. John's, said, "A lot of people have been hurt by this, and a lot of people have come together because of this. We've worked very hard to bring St. John's back together again." She went on to mention Father Madden. "We still really miss him," she said.

On November 26, 2007, federal prosecutors recommended that Father Fay be sentenced to at least forty-four months in prison. They stated that, based on federal sentencing guidelines, such a sentence was fair and just, because their investigation proved that Father Fay had stolen $1.3 million.

Tom Carson, the spokesman for the U.S. Attorney's Office, told reporters that "the final sentence is up to the judge. The guidelines are completely advisory."

Lawrence Hopkins objected to the $1.3 million figure and the recommended sentence. He filed papers with the court arguing that the federal prosecutors were double-counting. The actual figure was well below $1 million. And Father Fay had pled guilty to stealing only $400,000. Because of this, argued Hopkins, an adjustment should be made. He went on to make his own recommendation about sentencing: no jail time.

In support of his recommendation, Hopkins cited Father Fay's compassionate service to the dying and the needy. He included letters from former parishioners who spoke glowingly of Father Fay. Hopkins noted that Father Fay's crime was non-violent and did not warrant a severe sentence. Describing the dire condition of the priest's health, Hopkins ended by stating that "any significant sentence of incarceration will likely result in the defendant dying alone in prison. This would be an unduly harsh result in light of Michael Fay's lifelong commitment to comfort the dying."

Copies of medical records from Father Fay's doctor were included in the filing with the court. Hopkins didn't want the court to think that Father Fay wasn't already being punished more severely than any court could punish him.

At 3:30 in the afternoon, on December 4, 2007, Father

Michael Jude Fay was sentenced.

Outside the courthouse, the weather was cold, and a gray haze hung in the air, dampening everything it touched. That day Father Jude had resurrected the blond highlights in his hair. He wore a sling on his right arm. The result of a fall, explained his attorney.

Father Jude did not appear remorseful. In fact, his attitude was that of puzzled disbelief as he still did not believe he was guilty of anything. He had been the pastor of St. John's Church. In his mind, he had been entitled to do as he pleased with the church's money.

Looking at Father Jude, Judge Arterton said, "I'm going to call you Mr. Fay, if you don't mind."

Lawrence Hopkins rolled his eyes at the ceiling. The judge's words did not give him encouragement.

Father Jude pursed his lips and nodded at the judge, whose remark only reinforced his belief in his innocence. People did not understand the priesthood or what being a priest was all about. He was still a priest and always would be a priest, no matter how he was addressed.

Prosecutor Richard Schechter rose and went through the catalog of Father Jude's sins and crimes. He emphasized that the crimes demanded punishment of at least five to six years in prison.

Then it was Hopkins' turn to speak. "I vehemently disagree with the prosecutors double-counting," said Hopkins. "It's not only disreputable, it's ridiculous that they stoop to this measure to bolster their case." He looked around the courtroom, shaking his head. "If that's all it comes down to is numbers — and not people's lives — well . . . then why are we here?"

Looking at the judge, Hopkins said, "Your Honor, we

respectfully request that the sentence be composed of community service. There is very little chance of recidivism because of Father Fay's age and the status of his health."

Hopkins glanced down at his notes, then went on. "Regarding the restitution, Your Honor, we have no objection to the amount imposed. However, I hasten to say that we do not think there's any great chance of his being able to do that in any meaningful way. Whether you incarcerate him or not, any further restitution is academic."

Prosecutor Schechter rose and said, "On counsel's last point — that of restitution — I agree, Your Honor. There appears to be little chance of recouping anything more than has already been collected."

The amount of Father Jude's restitution was $250,000, far below the figure of $1.3 million Fay had stolen. So far, he had paid back $200,000. That was all he had.

Judge Arterton nodded. "Mr. Hopkins, I agree with you that Mr. Fay poses no risk of recidivism." She stared at Father Jude. "On the other hand, who would have ever suspected that for seven years you pilfered the offerings of the church?"

No one said anything. For five seconds, silence reigned in the courtroom.

Then the judge said, "Mr. Fay, do you have anything you'd like to say?"

Father Jude stood up. As he began to speak, the reasons for his almost magical abilities as a fundraiser and charmer became evident. His voice was dynamic with energy and persuasion. He related a story about beauty and ugliness and how both may be found in all people. In his story, Leonardo da Vinci was searching for human models for his famous painting *The Last Supper*. Finally, Leonardo found a man handsome enough to be the Apostle John, the one whom Jesus loved. Years later, when the painting was almost complete, Leonardo found a "most disheveled, even grotesque man — ugly enough to be Judas, the traitor." Father Jude said, "Leonardo was shocked when the grotesque man cried out, 'Years ago, I was the model for John.'"

He paused dramatically, making his point: for years he had been beautiful, raising money for the church, helping the dying with comfort and the needy with alms. Now, though, everyone considered him ugly and accused him of stealing the same money he had raised in the first place. He was still the same man.

The courtroom was silent as everyone thought about what he had said.

Father Jude turned to the judge. "Your Honor, I am deeply sorry for this whole situation," he said. "I accept full responsibility for my bad choices. Do not send me to prison. I am already in prison."

Without hesitation, Judge Arterton said, "Not even the collar can protect you from prison." She then addressed the standing-room-only crowd in the courtroom. "A sentence of probation would be impunity for a crime of enormity. Mr. Fay's crime was enormous both in the amount of money stolen and its impact on parishioners and on the issue of trust."

Judge Arterton looked at Father Jude's attorney. "Mr. Hopkins, your argument that Mr. Fay be spared prison because of his health problems did not persuade me. The Federal Bureau of Prisons has hospitals and hospice programs. Furthermore, your plea that Mr. Fay's past good deeds are enough to avoid prison has no validity in light of his crimes." She stuck out her jaw. "The opportunity to provide community service is still available. In our prisons, we have many needy people," she said.

Judge Arterton paused, arranging papers on her bench. "As to the matter of double-counting, as you call it, Mr. Hopkins," she said, "I agree with you. The amount is adjusted."

She glanced at her court clerk, who nodded. It was time.

Judge Arterton looked straight at Father Jude. "Mr. Fay, I sentence you to thirty-seven months in a federal correctional facility. You will begin serving your sentence on April 2, 2008."

The four-month gap between sentencing and actual prison time was so that Father Jude could complete his medical program. Judge Arterton was being merciful.

Inside the courtroom, admirers surrounded Father Jude like a whirlpool of sympathy.

His brother, Daniel Fay, was there, as was one of his sisters. Daniel told a reporter, "To say Mike must pay his dues, I argue he's paying his dues now. A prison sentence is the same as a life sentence."

Outside the courthouse, a handful of protesters circled and shouted out slogans. Most of them were former, disgruntled Catholics. Most of the protesters didn't know what they were mad about. They just knew they were mad. One of them, Robert Mulligan, said, "There's a great need in the church for openness and transparency to bring the church's practices into the 21st century."

When Father Jude read Mulligan's words in the newspaper the next day, he laughed out loud. "People just don't get it," he said to Cliff Fantini. "The Church has done things the same way for centuries. Why? Because it works. If this guy wants openness and transparency," he tapped the newspaper, "he's kidding himself. Transparency and power are incompatible." He laughed again and reread the article.

Father Jude and Cliff were in their luxury condo in Florida. The blue waves of the Atlantic Ocean pestered the white sand of the beach not fifty yards away. Father Jude had signed over his half of the condo as part of his obligation to make restitution. But since Cliff owned the other 50% of the property, it couldn't be sold without his permission. Which meant it wasn't going to happen.

On May 1, 2008, Bethany Derario — the former bookkeeper at St. John's Church — filed a lawsuit against the Diocese of Bridgeport and St. John's Parish. The suit stated that Ms. Derario had been the victim of whistleblower retaliation.

Her attorney thought they had a good case. He cautioned Bethany that anytime anyone took on the Roman Catholic Church bizarre things happened. But maybe the diocese would settle out of court.

Lawrence Hopkins was not only smart and a realist, he was a bulldog too. He filed motions for extensions three times. He petitioned the court to extend the date on which Father Fay had to report to prison. Each time he argued that Father Fay would die if he did not continue the experimental treatment for his prostate cancer. The treatment was not available in the Federal Bureau of Prisons. Which meant that the government would be responsible for his death. Additionally, argued Hopkins, by staying out of prison, Father Fay was saving taxpayers the cost of his cancer treatment.

"Father Fay is being treated with a drug known as MDV3100, Your Honor," Hopkins told the judge. "The doctors deem it promising. However, it cannot be administered by the Federal Medical Center."

Father Jude had been ordered to report to Butner, North Carolina, home of the Federal Medical Center. FMC was a prison and a hospital.

Prosecutor Schechter objected. "Mr. Fay does not deserve leniency," he said. "He has demonstrated no remorse for his actions, and his efforts at restitution have been negligible."

The extensions were granted.

On May 6, 2008, Father Fay arrived in court in New Haven. His attorney had filed another motion for extension, only this time Father Fay had to appear. He didn't have to say anything, just show up. His attorney did all the talking. Father Fay was noticeably thinner. His Armani suit drooped.

His oncologist showed up too. The doctor explained the course of treatment that Father Fay was undergoing and provided documentation. The judge ordered the documents sealed by the court. The doctor then said, "Your Honor, Father Fay's cancer has spread to his bones."

Judge Arterton said, "If it is determined that the Bureau of Prisons can administer your treatment, then you will report on July 8th. If they cannot . . . I will take further motions under advisement."

So far, Father Jude has served no jail time. He continues to live in Florida and New York, flying back and forth frequently. Where the money comes from no one knows.

If the doctor's prognosis of bone cancer was correct, then Father Jude is already a dead man. As of 2009, Father Jude is still alive — but God works in mysterious ways.

# CHAPTER 6

## SATAN TAKES
## A BRIDE

OUTSIDERS CALLED IT THE GLASS CITY because of its glass industry: windows, bottles, windshields, and glass art. Others called it the Auto Parts Capital of the World, a ridiculing reference to all the automotive-related companies in the city. Their huge, gray warehouses squatted like gigantic toads along the river.

The people of the Glass City called themselves Toledoans, a logical nickname since they lived in Toledo. Many of them were Roman Catholic, and good works were their stock in trade. One example of their piety was Mercy Hospital, which stood in Tiffin, an older but charming suburb. White stucco and red brick adorned the outside of the hospital building, while inside sick and suffering patients lay on clean white sheets where they were cared for by nuns trained as nurses, Sisters of Mercy.

Mercy Hospital had a small chapel for spiritual needs run by two chaplains, Father Jerome Swiatecki and Father

Gerald Robinson. Father Jerome, a tall and overweight priest, had family in the area. His family had money, so he was considered to be from "good stock." Father Gerald, with dark hair and pinched good looks, was slender and not very tall. Friendly and hardworking, both priests were well liked. Their parishioners trusted them, respected them, and heeded their spiritual guidance. They lived in quarters attached to the hospital. Their rooms were just down the hall from the chapel.

What no one knew was that Father Gerald was a Satanist.

Outside the chapel, a cold wind gusted beneath gray skies, which drizzled rain on this holy day — Good Friday. It was April 4, 1980, and inside the chapel Good Friday mass was being conducted by Father Gerald. He held a golden plate. On the plate, looking pure and white against the red velvet, rested the wafers of the host. The body of Christ. But before the host could be dispensed, it had to be blessed, which changed the wafers from yeastless flour and water into the actual body of Christ — the process called transubstantiation. Letting his right hand hover over the host, Father Gerald muttered words indistinctly.

On her aching old knees before him, with her head bowed and her eyes closed, seventy-one-year-old Sister Margaret leaned forward a bit, trying to hear the wondrous words. For they were words of power, divine words that fed her soul. Not only was this nonchalant priest mumbling, but also her hearing wasn't what it used to be.

Disappointment flooded through Sister Margaret when she couldn't hear the words. For a moment, righteous anger flared in her mind, but she quickly squashed her angry thoughts. Anger was a sin, and on Good Friday it was intolerable. She did wonder, however, what the other Sisters of Mercy thought of this lackadaisical performance. A number of them held similar poses on either side of her: resting on their knees, heads bowed in submission, eyes closed, and hands clasped in front of their hearts. For their hearts belonged to him, the Heart of the World, the savior.

Father Gerald moved down the line of worshippers, imparting the wafers of the host to each woman, these brides of Christ. As each lifted her head, opening her mouth to receive the bread, he dropped a wafer on a pink tongue, mumbling vaguely. Once again, Sister Margaret was annoyed. What was wrong with the man? Why did he cheat God so?

Finished with that chore, Father Gerald set the plate on the altar. Next to it stood a cup. With his back to the worshippers, he took the golden cup full of red wine, muttered something, then raised the cup to his pinched lips, swallowing a small sip of the wine. Carefully setting the cup back in its place on the altar, Father Gerald turned, raised his hands just above his head, and murmured a blessing. Then he walked out of the chapel.

Sister Margaret, stunned, remained on her knees, waiting for the priest to return. When he didn't, she glanced around at the sisters, seeking an explanation. She asked one of them, who was later interviewed, what was going on. Where was the liturgy of the word? The lessons, the prayers, the Lord's Prayer? This, in Sister Margaret's opinion, was sacrilege — an abomination! Someone needed to do something.

Taking a deep breath, Sister Margaret decided *she* would say something. Marching out of the chapel, she walked down the hall to where the priests lived. A dark-brown wood door confronted her. Raising her small fist, she gave the door three sharp raps.

Moments later the door opened. A pinched face stared at her. A few seconds later Father Gerald stepped aside, invited Sister Margaret to enter.

To this day, no one knows what she said. But she must have delivered a severe tongue lashing. When interviewed after the tragedy, Sister Sarah spoke of Sister Margaret's temper and bluntness. What is known for certain is this: the seventy-one-year-old nun wanted to know why Father Gerald had cut the service short. Why did he cheat God out of what was his?

The priest and the old nun had clashed before. She considered him lazy and inept, while he considered her straight-laced and insolent. His attitude was that he was the priest; she was the nun. Her job was to obey, not question. They would clash again and soon, for Sister Margaret was a chaste and stern woman. Only the next time would be the last time. Father Gerald's self-importance came out when the other nuns were interviewed by police investigators after the murder.

Margaret Ann Pahl entered the world of the living April 6, 1909. Her parents, Frank and Catherine Pahl, ran a farm and raised their children as good Catholics. They had five children, all girls.

In keeping with their pious upbringing, all but one of the girls became nurses. And of the four nurses, two entered the order known as the Sisters of Mercy, becoming the brides of Christ. They took vows of chastity and poverty and dedicated their lives to Jesus, to aiding the sick and suffering.

Margaret heard God's call while she was in high school. The course of her life was decided for her. Embracing the decision, she announced her intentions to her family. After her graduation, she would become a Sister of Mercy.

Before Margaret left for the convent, called Our Lady of the Pines, the teenaged girl gave away all her worldly goods. Each article of clothing was pressed and precisely folded. Jewelry and personal items, cleaned and polished, sparkled as if new. Spreading them all out on the bed and dresser in her meticulous room, she labeled each item with the name of its recipient.

"She was always neat like that, everything just so," said her sister Mary.

At Our Lady of the Pines, Margaret received religious training and then trained to become a registered nurse. Eventually appointed as director of Mercy Hospital's School of Nursing, she later took on additional duties as a hospital administrator. In both these jobs, she demanded exactness from those under her. Duties were to be performed in the manner prescribed by Sister Margaret and punctually. Daydreaming, gossiping, and lollygagging were not tolerated. Sister Margaret was definitely "old school."

In most of her photos, she wears her black nun's habit. There are a few, though, where she wears her formal bride of Christ habit. Pure white with a silver crucifix just below her bib. Unposed and slender, she smiles for the camera. Her face, shaped like an almond, carries fine features set in a pale complexion — almost like a pixy. There is no trace of vanity, self-consciousness, or cosmetics. The overall effect is one of inner beauty, spiritual strength, and firmness of mind.

The morning after her confrontation with Father Gerald, April 5th, ushered in Holy Saturday, the day before Easter.

Sister Margaret lived in a room in the staff's quarters on one of the upper floors of the hospital. Her alarm clock jingled at 5:00 a.m. To the east, a flush of light slowly seeped into the darkness hovering outside her window. Rising, she quickly bathed and dressed in her usual black nun's habit. Glancing around, she checked her room for tidiness. Nodding to herself, she decided it was acceptable.

Sister Margaret went downstairs, pausing at the hospital switchboard to check with the operator that everything was running smoothly. As she entered the cafeteria, she noted that it was 6:15 a.m. According to cafeteria workers, who were questioned later, Sister Margaret was on schedule but couldn't afford to dally or she would get behind. The chapel needed to be cleaned and the altar readied for the Easter mass. She didn't trust anyone else to do it. If she didn't do it, she knew it wouldn't be done correctly.

With small, quick steps, Sister Margaret paced over to the storage closet, where she placed cleaning cloths, cleaning solutions, and incense on a platter. She would light the incense after she cleaned to remove the smell of the chemical solutions used in cleaning. It would also purify the air of the sacred place, like the sweet odor of prayers rising to heaven.

Carrying her supplies, Sister Margaret walked down the hallway to the chapel, where she set them down on one of the burnished wooden pews. Looking around, she noted all that had to be done, then hurried back to the cafeteria for her breakfast. There was more to do than she had thought. One thing at a time, she told herself. That was the way to get things done.

Five minutes later, 6:20 a.m., Sister Margaret sat at her table in the cafeteria, eating half a grapefruit — one of the ones she liked so well, ruby reds they were called — and cereal with milk, no sugar. She allowed herself one cup of black coffee. With all that she had to do, she did not linger.

Finished, Sister Margaret returned her tray to the kitchen and, pausing, said good morning to the cafeteria cashier. "I can't talk," Sister Margaret said, "I'm on my way to the chapel." With that, she walked rapidly away, the heels of her flat black shoes clicking firmly.

By 6:45 a.m., Sister Margaret was back in the chapel, where she began dusting the sacristy, a small room also called the vestry. In it were stored sacred utensils used in the mass and the religious clothing — called vestments — worn by the priests as they performed holy services. The priests changed clothes in the sacristy before and after mass.

Ten minutes later, at 6:55 a.m., a uniformed figure passed by the chapel, tossing and then catching his key ring at the end of a stretch cord. This was Robert Wodarski, one of the hospital's security guards. He was making his morning rounds. Noting that the chapel doors were propped open and the lights inside were on, he did not stop, because this was normal. Someone, usually one of the nuns, or perhaps one of the chaplains, must be praying. If Wodarski had stopped and waited just thirty seconds, he would have encountered Father Gerald, who, dressed in his black cassock, having just left his quarters, was making his way down the hallway to the cafeteria to have his breakfast. But Wodarski did not stop. He continued making his rounds.

Father Gerald had not slept well. Anger at Sister Margaret's accusations had kept him up most of the night. The woman was insufferable. And he had just about had it with her. He'd taken a lot from her over the years, but enough was enough.

As Father Gerald passed the chapel, he saw the lights on, which wasn't surprising, but he thought he'd peek in and see who it was. He leaned in through the doorway and quickly surveyed the room. No one was there. Frowning, he was about to switch off the lights when, in the corner of his eye, he caught a movement. Walking in farther, he saw Sister Margaret in the sacristy. Her back was to him, and she was polishing something with a white rag. As she did, she hummed loudly.

Father Gerald recognized the tune — "A Mighty Fortress Is Our God." One of Martin Luther's old hymns, which he despised. Blue rage flared through the priest's body. Father Gerald stood motionless as vicious hatred sparked from him. Inside his head, something clicked with an audible snap. A thought, like a single germ, infected his mind. An evil smile touched the corners of his lips.

The timing was perfect for Father Gerald. Holy Saturday, the day before Easter; a nun, the bride of Christ; the chapel, the sanctuary of God — and no one around.

Father Gerald moved quickly back to the chapel doors, stepping softly, like a cat in a black dress. Closing the doors, he locked them. He then crept toward the sacristy. Through the doorway now. Sister Margaret hummed to her God, unsuspecting. Two more quick steps and he was right behind her.

Like a snake, he struck. Both his hands gripped her throat, steely fingers crushing the old nun's windpipe. The chalice Sister Margaret was polishing dropped with a clang on the wooden floor. Her neck arched back as the priest pulled and squeezed. Reaching up and back, she clasped the wrists that were squeezing the life from her. Then, fluttering her hands like a wounded bird, she twitched and went limp. With a black energy, the priest squeezed harder still, until his fingers almost met in the mashed flesh of the nun's neck.

Sunlight streamed in through the high window of the

sacristy, filling the room with a yellowish hue. The only sound in the room was the panting of the priest.

A nursing supervisor, one of the Sisters of Mercy, stood in the hallway outside the locked doors of the chapel. Bewildered, she checked her watch. It read 7:00 a.m. She couldn't fathom why the chapel wasn't open. It was always open by this time. She had wanted to pray before beginning her day's work. Looking around for someone to complain to, Sister Rose Byers finally shrugged and walked away.

Inside the sacristy, Father Gerald stared down at the crumpled body of Sister Margaret. Then, dropping to his knees, he grasped her under her arms and pulled the body until it was stretched out. He gently lowered her head to the floor and pressed her arms close to the sides of her body. Moving to her feet, he grabbed her thin ankles covered by black stockings and pulled her legs straight. Standing up, he looked down on her. Good. She looked like she would if she were in a coffin.

Turning, Father Gerald hurried to the locked doors, opened them, and locked them again from the outside with his key. Almost running, he walked rapidly back the way he had come. Entering his quarters, he made for his desk. There it was. A letter opener with an eight-inch blade. It looked more like a dagger than a common letter opener. Sliding the letter opener inside his cassock, he rushed back to the chapel, where, once again, he locked the doors behind him.

The Black Sabbath ritual was about to begin.

In the sacristy, Father Gerald took an altar cloth from one of the shelves. Standing over the stricken nun's body, he pulled the skirt of her habit up towards her neck. Then he pulled her black stockings and girdle down around her ankles. Kneeling beside the body, he spread the altar cloth over the nun's chest. He took his letter opener and began plunging its gleaming blade through the altar cloth into the murdered nun's torso. Like a chrome fang, the blade bit into pale flesh thirty-one times — in the pattern of an inverted cross.

A mockery of the Christian cross, the inverted cross is a blasphemy, symbolizing rejection of Jesus as the son of God and used by modern Satanists to signify their hatred of Christianity. The image comes from the verses in *Blood Wulfs Book: Chaos Lord*:

> Experience the nightmare of my desire.
> The stars glisten with my blood.
> I call unto you.
> I deny your faith.
> Live in the face of emptiness, yet
> You survive the details.
> I embrace your desire,
> And elevate violence to a sacred deed.
> You equip for immortality:
> I reap your soul for eternity.

Father Gerald Robinson was performing a ritualistic black mass, also known as the Black Sabbath. It was a mass for Satan. The elements of the black mass are intended to mock the death of Jesus Christ, sacrificed on Good Friday. On Holy Saturday, either a man or a woman was sacrificed, preferably a woman. On Easter Sunday, known to Satanism as Unholy Sunday, a woman or man was sacrificed followed by three days of fasting and chanting. Some groups sacrificed, cooked, and ate a human baby on Easter Sunday.

Sister Margaret, murdered on Holy Saturday, whose body

bore wounds in the pattern of an inverted cross, was Father Gerald's human sacrifice. She was killed to mock the God she loved, the God she served, the God she dedicated her life to as a bride of Christ.

By the time the priest finished his grisly ritual, the nun's blood was everywhere. Blood covered the once-white altar cloth, Sister Margaret's habit, and the floor. Father Gerald's hands were slick with the crimson fluid. On his black cassock, where the blood had splattered, bloomed dark spots, which felt buttery to the touch. The stains of human blood.

Time was running out, Father Gerald knew. But there was one more ritual to perform. The crowning touch, literally. He would baptize the old nun with her own blood, a kind of reverse Eucharist. In the Eucharist, wine represented the blood of Christ. In this instance, though, blood would stand for blood and black death.

Dipping his right thumb in a pool of blood on the floor, Father Gerald poised the dripping member over Sister Margaret's forehead. Then, with her own blood, he made the sign of an upside down cross on her brow. A scarlet horror of filth — the devil's mark.

It was done.

Nearly out of time. Someone would be coming soon. Rushing to the basin in the sacristy, Father Gerald rinsed both his hands and the diabolical weapon, the blood-covered letter opener, under a weak stream of water. Blood mixed with water splashed all over the white ceramic of the basin, making even more of a mess. Frantic with fear, he didn't have time to clean it up. Grabbing a linen cloth, he wiped his hands and the blade.

Drawing a deep breath, Father Gerald shook his head, trying to think clearly. Get out! He had to get out. He rushed to the locked doors, fumbling nervously with the lock for a moment. Finally. He flung the door open, dropping the damp linen cloth as he raced down the hallway to his quarters.

It was now 7:30 a.m.

At precisely that moment, Wardell Langston II stood talking to the receptionist. Her desk was just down the hall from the chapel. Wardell, one of the janitors, stopped talking and cocked his head. He heard something. From her expression, the receptionist did too. Running feet. It sounded as if someone was racing down the hallway, away from where he was, toward the priests' quarters.

Wardell thought it was flat-out weird. No one ever ran around there, especially not on a religious holiday weekend. Anyway, most of the building was empty. An ominous feeling washed over him, as if he was being slowly dipped in icy water. Something was wrong.

For an instant, Wardell gave thought to investigating. Then he reconsidered. He wasn't a hero by any means. Shrugging off his misgivings, he spent a few more minutes talking with the receptionist, then went back to work.

Thirty minutes later one of the Sisters of Mercy walked down the hallway to the chapel. Young and pretty, her name was Madelyn Marie Gordon. She wanted to pray. Just outside the doors, she noticed a white linen cloth on the floor. Picking it up, she sighed in relief to herself. Good thing Sister Margaret didn't find it. Someone would have been in big trouble.

Inside the chapel, as the nun walked past the organ, she changed her mind. First, she decided, she would make a phone call; then she would pray. There was a phone in the sacristy. She could use it. As she passed through the sacristy's doorway, a scene that could have been from Dante's *Inferno* greeted her. Sister Margaret posed in a pool of blood.

Screaming, the nun made the sign of the cross and raced out of the chapel to phone the police.

Sister Phyllis Gerold sat in her office working her way through piles of paperwork when she heard a series of piercing screams. The kind of screams that curdled your blood and ripped the very air, leaving it shimmering in agitation. She responded automatically, without any thought. Jumping up from behind her desk, she rushed out the door of her office, bumping her shoulder as she did. Racing down the hallway, she turned right and took the stairs two at a time down to the chapel.

Sister Phyllis flew through the open doors of the chapel and saw someone or something lying on the floor of the sacristy. She ran over to the doorway. Then she halted abruptly, almost falling backward. As she stared at the bloody spectacle, her hand jerked to her mouth. A silent scream escaped from her lips. Dear God! Her eyes felt as if they were bleeding, the sight hurt so.

"The horror of it, and the weirdness of it," she later said, paralyzed her. Then the feeling that she needed to be saved overwhelmed her. Only God could save her from such a horror. Stumbling back from the grisly scene, a single word repeated itself over and over in her mind. Why? Why?

When Detective William "Bill" Kina of the Toledo Police Department arrived at the murder site a short while later, he also wondered why. But, more importantly, he wanted to know who. Instructing two other detectives to begin gathering evidence in the sacristy, Detective Kina began interviewing anyone who had been near the chapel that morning.

Detective Ed Marok stepped gingerly into the sacristy. He

carried small plastic baggies and nail clippers. Kneeling next to the nun's bloody body, he clipped her fingernails short, placing the clippings in a baggie. He forgot to do two things: he failed to sterilize the nail clippers before using them, and he neglected to wear a surgical mask as he bent over the old nun's bloody corpse.

During his interviews, Detective Kina discovered some interesting information. An electrocardiogram technician, Leslie Kerner, stated that she had seen Father Gerald in front of the chapel doors at around 7:00 a.m. And Grace Jones, who worked in the hospital laboratory, recalled seeing Father Gerald scurry out of the chapel as she waited for the elevator at approximately 7:30 a.m.

Based on this information, along with the statements of others, the two detectives located Father Gerald and questioned him. Their first question was whether they could search his quarters. Father Gerald said that they could, that he had nothing to hide. While the questioning continued, other detectives searched his quarters, where they found a dagger-like letter opener. They bagged it as evidence.

Under questioning, Father Gerald denied any knowledge of the murder. He insisted that he hadn't left his quarters until he received a phone call from one of the hospital's administrators. The administrator told him that there had been a murder in the chapel. Prior to that, he had been in the shower. By the time he had got dressed and left his quarters, it was 8:15 a.m.

Detective Kina didn't believe Father Gerald. There was something strange about the priest. For one thing, he showed no emotion when he was told what had happened. His calmness was beyond belief, almost as if he didn't care. Another thing was that he didn't inquire who had been murdered.

Intuition told Kina that Father Gerald was the murderer. But he needed proof. So the interview continued. Kina was an experienced interrogator and knew how to intimidate people. Moving closer to the smallish priest, he spoke in a low voice. He implied that the priest knew something he wasn't sharing.

Again Father Gerald proclaimed he had nothing to do with any of it.

Detective Kina scoffed and kept repeating his questions. "I know you know something, Father," said Kina. "It will go easier for you if you tell me."

Finally, the little priest showed some emotion. Excitedly but reluctantly, he said that someone had confessed to him. He had been in the confessional listening to parishioners. A man had sat down on the other side of the screen. The man had told the priest that he had just killed a nun.

"I didn't say anything because what is revealed in confession is privileged," said Father Gerald. Glancing away from Kina's stare, the priest shrugged. "I'm not really sure that what I just told you is permissible," he added.

Detective Kina looked at the other policemen. Then he laughed. "C'mon, Father," he said and glanced at his wristwatch, a gold Timex with a gold stretch band. "It's not even ten o'clock yet, and you're telling me that between 8:15 — which is when you said you left your room — and now you had some guy confess murder to you?" Kina shook his head in disbelief. "Listen," he told the priest. "Anyone who just committed a murder is not going to stop off at the nearest church and confess his crime. No way. He's going to be in an all-fired hurry to get as far away as he can, as fast as he can."

"I'm telling you someone confessed to me," said the priest, looking down and to the left. "I know what I heard."

"I know what I just heard too, Father. And that's not the truth, is it?" said Kina.

Father Gerald licked his lips and nodded his head. "No, it's not," he admitted in a whisper.

"Then why did you say it?"

"I felt like I had to say something," he said and squirmed in his chair. "You don't believe me, and you keep pressuring me." He looked away. "I gave in to the pressure, I guess. It was a mistake. I'm sorry I lied to you."

An instance of what can only be described as burlesque — a prime specimen of travesty — occurred four days later. Father Gerald Robinson and Father Jerome Swiatecki celebrated Sister Margaret Pahl's funeral mass.

It was April 9, 1980. Sister Margaret died on Saturday; they buried her on Wednesday. Another way to look at it: Father Gerald murdered her on Holy Saturday; then he presided over her funeral three days after Easter, which was also her birthday. One more day and she would have turned seventy-two on the day of Jesus' resurrection. Instead, she had been served up as a human sacrifice.

Carrying umbrellas, hundreds of people gathered at St. Bernadine's Chapel. Overhead roiled and rumbled black clouds like dark drapes hanging from heaven. Each time the wind gusted the large metal cross on the roof trembled and shook as if seized by an epileptic fit. Inside the chapel, Father Jerome made pushing movements with his right arm, from which dangled a silver orb on a chain. As it swayed from side to side, smoke streamed from holes. Called a censer or thurible, incense burns inside it. Even to the initiated, it is eerie. The venting smoke was an *axis mundi*, the path of escape from time and space into the eternal and unconfined. At the same time, it was a picture of prayers going up, an invitation for God's presence here and now.

Many of those present wondered where God had been four days earlier.

A gust of wind argued rudely with the metal cross on the roof. With a booming noise, the front doors of the chapel burst open. Cold wind dashed in, herding dead leaves along the red carpet. Someone or something had entered the chapel.

Some thought that old vagabond — the devil himself — had blown in, flamboyant entries being his specialty. Not Paul Casebere, a relative of Sister Margaret; he thought God or one of his angels had made an entrance. An angry one. "It wouldn't have surprised me one bit," he said, "if that roof had come off the church."

The doors were shut, and the funeral mass continued.

Two weeks later Father Gerald Robinson agreed to take a polygraph test at the police station. A few days after that he took another polygraph test, this time with a polygrapher hired by the Catholic diocese.

The police wanted to interview Father Gerald again. He and Father Jerome drove down to the station. Father Jerome wasn't allowed into the interrogation room. But before Father Gerald went in, Father Jerome looked him in the eyes, pleading with him. "Just tell the truth," he said. "Just tell the truth."

Detective Kina didn't think it was a coincidence. He wondered if the lie about the killer confessing to Father Gerald wasn't the other way around. Had Father Gerald confessed to Father Jerome? Was that why Jerome was urging Gerald to tell the truth? If it was, it didn't work, because the little priest stuck to his story.

Later Detective Kina presented his gathered evidence to the district attorney. "The physical evidence includes fingernail clippings, the letter opener, and the blood-stained altar cloth," he said. "The lab people say the letter opener is consistent with the puncture wounds on the nun's body."

The district attorney nodded, sitting behind his desk.

"I've also got statements from two witnesses which place the priest near the chapel at the time of the murder. Other statements indicate a history of dislike, if not downright hostility, between the deceased and the priest," said Kina, his fingers tapping a thick folder on the desk. "And what's more damning is the priest's lack of an alibi and the fact that he lied." Kina held his hands out as if astonished. "Some cock-and-bull story about someone confessing to the murder. But of course he can't tell us who because of the sanctity of the confessional." He paused. "He took two polygraphs. He failed the first one, and the second one was inconclusive. Which, by definition, means he failed again." Kina looked straight at the man seated in front of him. "He's lied repeatedly."

Smiling, the district attorney looked up at the standing detective. "Anything else?"

"Yeah, there is," said Kina in a definite tone.

"Which is?"

Kina leaned forward. "My gut feeling is that this is our guy." He planted his index finger firmly onto the file folder.

Nodding with respect, the district attorney said, "You're probably right. But I can't use your gut instinct in court." Reaching forward, he picked up the file folder and, leaning back in his chair, leafed through it. Sitting upright again, the prosecutor pushed the file folder back to Kina. "Unfortunately, this isn't enough evidence to get an indictment."

"You're kidding me," said Kina, not wanting to pick up

the folder.

"No, I'm not," said the district attorney. "Any judge will toss it right out." Frowning, he paused. "Look, we are dealing with a Catholic priest, which, as you well know, means we are putting the whole Catholic Church on trial. And that's almost impossible. Additionally, this murder has all the earmarks of a ritual killing, some kind of nut-case thing. No one is going to believe a priest had anything to do with it."

Twenty-three years later, on June 11, 2003, in the offices of the Toledo Catholic diocese, a letter arrived. It was opened and read. Within minutes, the diocese sent for Thomas Pletz, lead legal counsel for the diocese. After Pletz read the letter, he sighed heavily and told the bishop that the legal ramifications to the diocese and the Catholic Church were enormous. Nevertheless, they had a legal responsibility to forward a copy of the letter to the Placer County District Attorney's Office. The next day Pletz fulfilled his legal responsibilities.

The letter, written by a woman named Mary, alleged that she had suffered sexual, physical, and psychological abuse when she was a child. The abuse had gone on for years, until she was old enough to realize what was happening to her. Her abusers, diocesan priests, had forced her to participate in ritualistic sexual perversions — Satanic rituals — in which Mary had been the victim. The allegations went on at length and provided detailed accounts and descriptions. These were not reckless accusations by someone looking for a cash settlement. Rather, they were the diary of a ravaged and wounded soul.

At the District Attorney's Office, the forwarded copy of the letter went without attention for six long months. The allegations were old, really old. Decades old. And unsubstantiated. Besides, there were present-day, compelling crimes to deal with.

Somebody — whether from the D.A.'s office, an ugly gray building, or from the diocesan office, a beautiful white marble structure — talked too much. At last, a clerical abuse support group in Toledo found out about the letter. They contacted the attorney general of Ohio and raised a big stink. The attorney general appointed one of his go-to people, special prosecutor Mary Bates (a real bulldog, according to her fellow prosecutors), to investigate the letter.

The special investigation team contacted Mary, the author of the letter. She agreed to speak with them. After the interview with Bates, the investigation team sat in stunned silence. Her story rang true. In fact, it thundered honesty.

In the course of the interview, Mary had named Father Gerald Robinson as one of her abusers.

One of the special investigators thought he recognized that name. It tickled his memory banks for some reason. After he let it bounce around his brain for a while, he remembered why. It was the name of that little priest down at the hospital who had been a prime suspect in a bizarre homicide — some poor old nun — years ago. The murder was bizarre because it, too, smelled of a Satanic cult killing. The body had been stretched out in a pose, and there was a crazy number of stab wounds on it in the pattern of an upside down cross. Real hellish stuff.

Clearing his throat, he told the other members of the team what he remembered.

Special Prosecutor Mary Bates listened carefully. Intrigued by what she heard, she decided to give the tree a shake and see what fell out. In keeping with her nickname of Bulldog Bates, she clamped her jaws. Forensic techniques had taken five giant steps forward in the past twenty-three years. So she brought in a group of experts and turned them loose on the evidence in cold storage: the altar cloth, the letter opener, and the blood samples.

Father Gerald, no longer a chaplain, was semi-retired now. He was a parish priest and lived in a nice house, which he owned along with his brother. Bates ordered it searched. A warrant was obtained, and the team drove to the house. Father Gerald was flabbergasted at the number of people standing on his front porch. Cops. They all looked the same. They presented their warrant and entered the house.

Just inside the door of his own house, now holding the warrant, stood Father Gerald. Sixty-five years old now, his cheeks had plumped a bit, so he didn't look as if someone had pinched his face. He couldn't believe it. Twenty-three years! But he wasn't worried. He had been innocent then, and he was innocent now.

After an extensive search, the team found two interesting things.

First was a pamphlet with the ominous title of *The Occult*. Many passages in the pamphlet had been underlined. One of the marked passages spelled out the manner in which the body of "an innocent" was used as an altar. However, the pamphlet had been published by a Catholic group as a warning against the dangers of occult involvement. On the one hand, it didn't really prove anything. On the other hand, it was coincidental to the point of being spooky, especially when the particulars of Sister Margaret's death were considered. Warning bells went off in a lot of heads.

Even spookier were the photos they found in the house. Hundreds of them. Photos of corpses lying in coffins. Some looked to be old, as in "old as dirt." Others exhaled a foreign breath, as if they were from another country. Maybe Europe, maybe not, but definitely gothic in a grotesque sense. None of the police officers knew what to make of it. But chills crawled up and down their spines because the photos were everywhere in the house. They hung in their frames in rows on the walls and perched atop every available flat surface. Unless blindfolded, it was impossible not to look at the gruesome things.

One of the younger officers walked over to Detective Kina. "This is worse than being in a graveyard at night," he said, indicating the photos with a nod of his head. "At least in a graveyard they're not staring back at you."

"I know," said Kina.

The policeman moved off, muttering something under his breath.

They took photos of the photos and bagged a few of them as physical evidence, along with the pamphlet. Getting into their unmarked Crown Victorias, they left. Father Gerald stood on his front porch, still holding the search warrant. He looked lost.

A few minutes later he went back into his house and called an attorney, Alan Konop, an old friend and a member of his parish.

Back at the police station, one of the analysts unearthed lore about the photos found in the priest's house. Photographing corpses in coffins was a late-Victorian custom. During the days of Queen Victoria, people in England were maniacal about remembering their dead family members. Part of that process included photos. They would photograph the corpse in its coffin, then frame the photo and keep it. Pretty weird stuff.

But as far as anyone could tell, it had no bearing on Father Gerald's innocence or guilt. It did, though, indicate an abnormal obsession with the dead. Add to that the fact that these were not photos of his dead family members, and all that was left was . . . Well, what was left? The guy was creepy.

Special Prosecutor Mary Bates thought the priest was a lot more than creepy. She thought he was guilty of murder. So did the Lucas County district attorney. Standing before the grand jury, he presented his evidence. After he finished, the grand jury decided to indict the priest for murder.

On April 23, 2004, police officers arrived again at the home of Father Gerald Robinson. Charged with the murder of Sister Margaret Pahl, he was booked and incarcerated in the Lucas County Jail, where he was placed in protective custody. Exchanging his black suit, black clergy shirt, and white collar for jail-issued clothing, he was then assigned to a small, private cell and kept under constant surveillance.

John Thebes, Alan Konop, and John Callahan, who all practiced private criminal law, formed Father Gerald's defense team. They immediately went to work, contacting the District Attorney's Office to determine the charges. In effect, this was the beginning of the negotiation process, which took place in every criminal case. Unfortunately, they quickly realized, there was little room for negotiation. The state had a strong case.

The charge was aggravated murder. Bail was set at $200,000, and, because of the gravity of the charge, either the entire amount had to be paid in cash or property equity worth twice that amount had to be put up as collateral. If not, no bail bondsman would touch it. There was too much risk of flight.

Father Gerald and his brother, Thomas, owned the house in which the priest was arrested. Thomas also owned another house. Both houses were put up as collateral. Two other houses owned by parishioners Gary Glowski and Dorothy Sieja were also put up. As members of Father Gerald's church, they believed their priest was innocent, incapable of such a dreadful act.

On May 3, 2004, a small army of people waited outside the Lucas County Jail. Supporters of the priest milled about, waiting impatiently. A legion of television reporters and newspaper writers migrated through the crowd like sharks, looking for someone who knew something new. Photographers bulging with cameras, lenses, and light meters snapped thousands of pictures. Television cameramen vied for the best spots from which to film. They were all waiting for Father Gerald.

A wave of sound and motion pushed through the crowd. There he was. Father Gerald walked out of the jail. On one side of him, her arm hooked through his, walked his sister-in-law. She wore a white jacket and sunglasses. On his other side, in a dark suit, his eyes invisible behind aviator sunglasses, walked his attorney, John Callahan.

A small cheer from his supporters greeted the priest. The media swarmed toward him, yelling questions, pushing microphones in front of him. Cameras clicked and whirred non-stop.

The attorney motioned people out of their way. Without stopping or making any comment, the trio entered an SUV and drove off. The vehicle headed for the Scott Park Banquet Room, where a release celebration had been planned.

Arriving at the banquet room, Father Gerald and seventy-five of his friends and parishioners ate and drank to his health and innocence. On the surface, everyone was happy and relaxed, but there was a subdued energy swimming beneath, for everyone felt the pressing shadow of the looming trial.

The party was over. People were drifting out, pausing out front of the banquet room to chat. Standing outside was a middle-aged woman. Her face glowed with intensity. In one hand, she clutched a doll dressed as a nun. "Killer," screamed Paulina Cleveland, holding the doll at arm's length. "Nun killer!"

Shocked into silence, no one knew what to do. Then they began to walk away from the woman, ignoring her.

Paulina bristled at the lack of response. Angry, she wanted a fight. Paulina marched up the steps and through the doors into the banquet room. Halting, she faced the crowd still inside. Thrusting out the doll, she shouted, "I am here for Sister Margaret. She is the one who suffered. Justice for Sister Margaret!" As her eyes glanced wildly around, she spotted the priest. "Murderer! Nun killer!" she shrieked at him.

Then Paulina turned on her heel and walked back toward the front doors. As she approached them, she paused and glared at a man standing by the doors. His name was Rick Napierala. She waited for him to open and hold a door for her. When he didn't, she hit him with the doll. Rick stepped back, looking at the crazy woman. She raised the doll to hit him again. Rick reached out and plucked it from her hand.

"Give it back!" screamed Paulina. "Give it back to me! Right now!"

"No," said Rick.

Paulina launched herself at him. As he tried to avoid her, she clutched at his coat. He turned to get away, but the woman wouldn't stop. She pulled his coat off, tearing his shirt pocket as her hands yanked back and down. Then she was on him. As he turned to fend her off, the hellcat clawed his face with both her hands. His eyeglasses crashed to the floor. Rick lurched back out of her reach, turned, and walked by one of the banquet tables. Paulina rushed to the table, picked up a pitcher of ice water, and threw it at him. He couldn't believe this was happening. As he stood there trying to decide what to do, the woman snatched her doll out of his hand and flounced out the doors.

Members of the media idled across the street, hoping to interview the priest. They had seen the woman and heard her shouts. As they approached her, she brandished the doll and screamed, "To honor Sister Margaret, I will go to jail." Then she left.

Later, after the uproar was over, Rick Napierala filed a police report about the episode. Assault and battery charges were lodged against Paulina Cleveland.

Four days later Father Gerald stood before Judge Patrick Foley and pled not guilty to the charge of aggravated murder. No one expected anything else.

For the next seven months, both sides prepared for trial. Witnesses were lined up, discovery hearings took place. During the discovery hearings, the prosecutors and the defense counselors exchanged all evidence and information. The prosecutors were meticulous because they didn't want to risk a mistrial for any reason.

After reviewing all the evidence, the district attorney, on December 31, 2005, reduced the charge against Father Gerald from premeditated murder to murder. "The killing was not premeditated, in the state's opinion." But it was still murder.

At the end of April 2006, the legal battle started. Many viewed it as the age-old struggle between the powers of good and the forces of evil — light against dark. Father Gerald was now sixty-eight years old.

Once the jury was selected, the trial began. Forty-one witnesses were scheduled to give testimony. Since there were no eyewitnesses to the murder, all the evidence presented during the course of the trial would be circumstantial. Before the law, except for eyewitness testimony, all evidence is circumstantial. The question the jury needed to answer was this: under what circumstances did the evidence get there (at the scene of the crime)?

Lucas County's prosecutors were Dean Mandros, Larry Kiroff, and J. Christopher Anderson. Young, smart, and aggressive, all three were very capable. Their job was simple: to convince twelve jurors that the priest was guilty of a horrifying murder, the murder of seventy-one-year-old Sister Margaret, a nun who had devoted her life to caring for others. The prosecutors were dedicated too — to justice and to putting away criminals for a long time.

They called their first witness. A gray-haired woman walked forward, eighty-two-year-old Sister Rose Byers. Now retired, Sister Rose was still very sharp.

"What was your job at Mercy Hospital in the year 1980?" asked Kiroff.

"I was a nurse," she said, pride in her voice. "I worked the night shift, usually."

"And what do you recall about the morning of April 5, 1980?" said Kiroff. "Anything unusual take place?"

"Yes," said Sister Rose. "Every morning for eighteen years, after I finished my night shift, I would go to the chapel to pray." She glanced at the jury, who listened intently. "That morning," Sister Rose went on, "was the first morning I could not get in."

"Into the chapel, you mean?" said Kiroff.

"Yes. I thought maybe they had closed it for some reason. The next day was Easter, so maybe they were getting it ready or something."

"What did you do then?"

"I left. I had some things I needed to do before I went off duty."

"And then what happened?" said Kiroff.

"Well, later, a few hours later, I learned that Sister Margaret was killed in the chapel," said Sister Rose, shaking her head. "It was horrible."

"What time was she murdered, do you know?"

Sister Rose leaned forward. "At almost exactly the same moment I was trying to get into the chapel to pray. She was probably in there dying, if not already dead." Tears streamed down her cheeks.

"How did you react when you learned about Sister Margaret's murder?"

"I was stunned," said Sister Rose, dabbing at her eyes with a tissue. "I couldn't believe it."

The next witness was retired police officer Ed Marok.

Father Gerald's defense attorneys contended that, since the source of DNA material under the dead nun's nails was not Father Gerald's, it pointed to the presence of another, unidentified killer.

Prosecutor Kiroff disagreed.

Officer Marok admitted, under oath, that he forgot to sterilize the nail clippers. He also stated that he was not wearing a surgical mask when he worked.

"Do you know whether you sneezed?" asked Kiroff.

"I don't recall," Marok said.

Kiroff turned to the jury. "That means that, because of a simple human mistake, the DNA could have come from Officer Marok or one of the medical personnel who arrived later. It does not point to another man, an anonymous killer," explained Kiroff. He then turned to Marok. "Thank you, Officer Marok," said Kiroff.

Reverend Jeffrey Grob came to the stand when called. An expert in exorcism, demonic worship, and ritual sacrifices, he was the associate canonical vicar for the Archdiocese of Chicago.

"Based on what you know and have been told, Father, what kind of person would you say committed the murder of Sister Margaret?" asked J. Christopher Anderson.

"Someone with specialized knowledge of religious rites and symbols," said Grob. "Either a priest or a seminarian."

"Not a layperson, then?"

"No. Definitely not. The use of the altar cloth, the baptism with blood — all indicate someone with a thorough understanding of the faith."

"So you're saying it would have to have been someone from the clergy?" asked Anderson, raising his eyebrows.

"Yes," said Grob.

"Which aspect of the murder — the ritual — leads you to believe this was a ritual killing, a sacrifice?" asked Anderson.

Sighing audibly, Grob said, "Where does one begin? In the eyes of the Church, a nun is a virgin wed to God, and when her body was left half naked, well, whoever did it was defiling the bride of Christ."

"So this is an example of religious profanation?"

"Of course, yes. A profaning of what is holy and pure. This is a sign — a hallmark, if you will — of Satanic worship." He paused and twisted his fist for the jury. "You take innocence, and you destroy it or mock it."

"What about the upside down cross carved in her flesh?" asked Anderson.

"It's used in Satanic ceremonies as an affront to the sacred. And the punctured altar cloth tells me that there was a desire to penetrate the holy with evil."

"What, to you," asked Anderson, "is the worst part of this horrendous murder?"

"The fact that the murder took place in the sacristy. That is where the Eucharist is kept. In the eyes of the Church, the murder took place in the presence of Jesus because Jesus is the Eucharist," said Grob. Then he added, "An act of pure evil."

"Okay," said Anderson, gathering his thoughts. "Now, Father, what happens to a priest who hears a confession, then reveals that confession to authorities?"

"Canon law is clear," said Grob. "Priests cannot reveal the identity of the confessor, nor may they discuss the content of any confession."

"What happens? I mean, what does the Church do if such an act takes place?" said Anderson.

"The penalty is excommunication," said Grob in a weighty voice.

"And what is the penalty if a priest reveals the contents of a confession, . . ." said Anderson, walking away from the priest, then turning back dramatically, ". . . and he is lying?" Anderson dropped his chin and looked at Father Gerald, who was seated at the defense table.

"The same penalty," said Grob, staring straight ahead.

John Thebes, one of Father Gerald's attorneys, took the

floor. "I am reminded," said Thebes, "of the gospel account of Saint Peter, who, three times, insisted he did not know Jesus." Cocking his head, he looked at Father Grob. "Under stress, Saint Peter denied Christ, did he not?"

"Well done," said Grob in admiration.

"And did not Peter become the pope of our Church?" asked Thebes.

"That is what we believe," said Grob, nodding.

Thebes faced the jury. "Stress, ladies and gentlemen," he said, "can make a man do strange things. Especially when he feels bullied by police officers." Opening his arms as if asking for understanding, he continued, "Lying under the stress of coercion does not make one a murderer."

Next the jurors watched a videotaped interview. In the video, Father Gerald is questioned by Investigator Thomas Ross of the Prosecutor's Office. Taken in 2004, just after his arrest, Father Gerald appears impassive and disinterested.

At one point in the video, Ross shouts at the priest. "Why are you smirking at me? This is serious."

"I am not smirking. I was not there," says Father Gerald in a subdued voice.

Later in the video, Father Gerald tells Ross, "They told me I was a suspect because I was too calm. They told me I didn't respond normally, like a murderer would. But I just don't have that in me — to holler and scream and demand my rights."

Most damning, at one point in the video, Father Gerald states that he did not have a key to the chapel sacristy.

Ross then tells him, "Two of the nuns at the hospital say that you and Father Jerome — that both of you have keys."

Father Gerald replies, "I am not lying."

The first forensic witness to take the stand was Paulette Sutton. A forensic scientist, she was one of only five experts in the country authorized to perform blood stain pattern analysis. Slender and pretty, an air of competence traveled with her.

Kiroff led her through a number of technical questions and asked about her qualifications. Then he got to the point.

"Is this the murder weapon?" Kiroff asked her, holding up a plastic bag. In the bag was the letter opener. Sitting like statues, the jurors stared at it.

"Traces of blood from the domed roof and columns on the medallion clearly made an imprint on the cloth," she said, gesturing toward the projection screen on the wall. "If another object made it, it would have to be basically the same shape, same size, and same configuration."

Kiroff gazed at the jury. He could see they got it. He wouldn't have to explain the astronomical odds of such a coincidence occurring.

The prosecutors called their next witness. A handsome man with Asian features walked forward to take his place in the witness box. His eyes sparkled with vitality, and he smiled as he took the oath to tell the truth.

"Would you tell us your name, sir?" asked Kiroff.

"Henry Lee," said the man.

Everyone in the packed courtroom sat up straighter. Dr. Henry Lee, the famous forensic scientist, was in Ohio. He'd been on TV in the O.J. Simpson trial and had consulted in the JonBenet Ramsey case.

Kiroff began questioning the celebrated scientist about the letter opener. The prosecutor directed everyone's attention to the projection screen showing an enlargement of a blood stain on an altar cloth. "Dr. Lee," he asked, holding up the plastic bag containing the dagger-like letter opener, "did this letter opener leave that blood stain on the altar cloth, the one depicted on the screen?"

"All I can conclude," said Dr. Lee, "is 'similar to.'"

Kiroff handed Dr. Lee the plastic bag. Dr. Lee examined it. He had already seen it and done a number of tests on it. "The small medallion on the side of the opener is consistent with the stain that was left on the cloth," Dr. Lee said, pointing to the dime-sized ornament on the side of the letter opener. "However, I cannot come here to tell you this pattern is produced exactly like this." Dr. Lee pointed at the screen. "Again, all I can say is 'similar to.'"

Investigators had determined that the letter opener was a souvenir purchased by Father Gerald Robinson in Washington, D.C. It had a representation of the U.S. Capitol on the medallion. He had chaperoned a church tour group many years ago.

Kiroff tilted his head back a little, gazing intently at Dr. Lee. "Dr. Lee, was the letter opener you hold in your hand the weapon that made the thirty-one stab wounds in the body of Sister Margaret Pahl?"

"The wounds are consistent with this object," he said. "But I cannot tell you more than 'similar to.' This object could have made the wounds. But I cannot say that this specific object produced them." He smiled apologetically.

Kiroff nodded. "Thank you for your expertise, Dr. Lee. Now, what tests did you perform on the letter opener?"

Turning toward the jury, Dr. Lee said, "I used certain chemicals — called reagents — to draw out very small specks of blood in the cloth. This sharpens the edges of the stain." He pointed to the screen. "As you can see, the ring shape is evident. And the semi-circle stains at the top are consistent with the roof lines of the building on the medallion."

"So," said Kiroff, speaking to the jury. "This weapon or one exactly like it was the murder weapon."

Turning to Dr. Lee, Kiroff asked, "In your expert opinion, Dr. Lee, how was Sister Margaret killed?" He handed Dr. Lee a number of police photos.

Dr. Lee took a magnifying glass from his pocket and began inspecting the photos. Looking up at the jury, he said, "You never know when you're going to be called to a crime scene, and you can't carry a microscope with you," he said, laughing.

The jurors smiled and chuckled.

In a few moments, Dr. Lee said, "She appears to be the victim of a quick attack. She was strangled from behind, disabled or knocked down pretty quickly on the floor. Most of the stabbing was inflicted afterwards."

"Thank you, Dr. Lee," said Kiroff. He walked back to his seat, nodding to the defense table.

Father Gerald's attorney, Konop, spent five minutes questioning Dr. Lee. He emphasized the possibility that a similar weapon could have made the wounds. It could not be established that this particular letter opener had been the murder weapon. Reasonable doubt existed. Which meant, said Konop, that Father Gerald had not been there. He was not the murderer.

On the last day of the trial, three witnesses gave testimony.

Leslie Kerner, the EKG technician, said, "I saw him outside the chapel. It was him and not Father Jerome, because Father Robinson was shorter and had more hair, and Father Jerome was larger and didn't have much hair."

Grace Jones said, "I was waiting for the elevator at about 7:30 a.m. on that morning. I saw Father Gerald coming out of the chapel carrying something."

"What did you do?" Larry Kiroff asked.

"I nodded, and he nodded and then went on," said Grace.

"Which father?" said Kiroff, looking around the court-room.

She indicated the defense table, where Father Gerald sat. His face was blank. "The one over there," she said.

The last witness was Dr. Jack Baron, who, twenty-six years earlier, was the chief medical resident at Mercy Hospital.

"I saw a man dressed in priest's garb in the hallway," said Dr. Baron.

"Why were you in the hallway?" asked Kiroff.

"I was on my way to see if I could do anything for the victim. I had just learned that something terrible had taken place. There was a call over the public address system for medical emergency help in the chapel," explained Dr. Baron.

"Are you sure it was that man?" asked Kiroff, pointing to Father Gerald.

"Yes," said Dr. Baron. "Same age, build, and hair color. I didn't know him by name, though."

"So you passed him in the hallway?"

"Yes."

"Did you say anything to him or he to you?"

"No. But he was within ten feet of me, looking over his shoulder and going in the opposite direction."

Attorney Alan Konop rose and questioned Dr. Baron. "I hold here the police report," Konop said, raising the pages for all to see. "There is no record of you having passed any priest in any hallway." He gave the pages to Dr. Baron.

Dr. Baron glanced through the report. "No, there isn't."

"And isn't it true, Dr. Baron," said Konop, "that you could not identify Father Gerald in photographs shown to you by the police in 1980?"

"That is correct," said Dr. Baron.

At the end of nine days of testimony, the prosecutors rested the state's case, declaring that all the evidence proved Father Gerald Robinson had murdered Sister Margaret Pahl. Defense attorneys countered by insisting that all the evidence presented was vague, and inconclusive by any reasonable standards, and that someone else, whose DNA was present at the scene, was responsible for the murder. According to the defense, evidence stronger than any reasonable doubt existed. Therefore, the jury in good conscience was obligated to acquit Father Gerald. Under the law, he had to be set free.

Realistically, throughout the trial, the defense attorneys had little to work with. They could only offer obscure theories and try to distract the jury from the increasing pile of damning evidence. If they confused the jurors enough, perhaps they could at least get a mistrial.

The jury moved to the deliberation room. Six hours later the jury returned their verdict. Guilty.

Judge Thomas Osowik immediately sentenced Father Gerald Robinson to fifteen years to life. As the sentence was pronounced, Father Gerald showed no emotion. A blank face — void and without form — looked back at the judge.

Bishop Leonard Blair of the Toledo diocese issued a statement. "Let us hope that the conclusion of the trial will bring some measure of healing for all those affected by the case as well as for our local church. The diocese has remained steadfast in the work of the Church and its ministries throughout this trial, and will continue to do so." Then he added that Father Gerald's status was that of a retired priest and that Father Gerald continues to be barred from any public ministry. At no point did the bishop express an opinion about Father Gerald's innocence or guilt. And, unsurprisingly, there was never any mention of the black mass, ritual sacrifice, or devil worship.

Denial is one of the easiest sins.

Two days after the trial, attorneys for Father Gerald Robinson filed an appeal with the Ohio 6th District Court of Appeals. In their appeal, they accused the prosecutors of having sensationalized the case by characterizing Father Robinson as "the Anti-Christ" and claiming that Pahl had been killed in a Satanic ritual. The evidence was tainted, stated the attorneys, by the passage of twenty-four years, and several key witnesses for the defense had died. After due reflection, the 6th District Court ruled against the appeal.

On January 16, 2009, Father Robinson's attorney filed a second appeal. The new motion asked the court to vacate Father Robinson's conviction, and allow a new trial. The motion stipulated the existence of another murder suspect, who had another motive, along with a murder weapon. Attorney John Donahue stated that sixty different pieces of evidence, never submitted during trial, contradicted the state's theory that Father Robinson was the murderer. "These sixty pieces of evidence are in a number of different forms. Some of them are police reports from 1980. Some of the evidence is contained in witness statements from 1980. There are affidavits," explained Donahue.

The District Court has not yet ruled on the second appeal. However, Dean Mandros, who was the lead prosecutor, stated in unequivocal terms that the state is confident the court will toss the appeal out.

Father Gerald tarries in a maximum-security prison. His cell is six feet by ten feet. On his next birthday, he will be seventy-one, the same age as Sister Margaret Pahl when she died and, as the bride of Christ, went to be with her bridegroom.

Father Gerald still insists he is innocent. But most criminals do because in their own minds they are. All requests for interviews with Father Gerald are turned down, so no one knows how, where, when, and why he got involved in Satanism.

One thing is certain: where he is — in prison — he has a lot of time to pray.

# SOURCES

The primary sources for this book emerged from many conversations, interviews, court transcripts, formal complaints, and depositions. Many are quoted here, but those that are not still contributed vitally to the text. In addition to these sources, I have referred to countless articles, studies, and a few important books.

The members of the clergy who agreed to speak did so only because I was a priest who had been convicted of embezzlement and spent time in jail. Where individuals are quoted but not named, it is because they agreed to speak only if not identified.

The following sites proved priceless in obtaining documents: Public Record Retriever Network; Black Book Online; Public Record Finder; Factiva; LexisNexis; xrefer; and People Tracker.

Chapter 1: "Making Bank." The *Palm Beach Post* and the

*New York Post* ran in-depth articles on Father Guinan and Father Skehan. Court transcripts and documents (the formal complaints) along with personal recollections were vital to this chapter.

Chapter 2: "Sins of the Fathers." Ellen Joan Pollock's book *The Pretender* proved invaluable in this chapter, especially regarding Martin Frankel. *Social Diary* provided interesting information about Thomas Corbally. SEC documents detailed the financial funny business that investigators discovered, and the lengthy complaint filed by the U.S. government clarified many of the intricate connections. Court transcripts were valuable resources, as were personal recollections.

Chapter 3: "Father Flim Flam." Articles published by the Catholic League assisted in this chapter. Primary sources were court transcripts, formal complaints filed in court, and personal recollections.

Chapter 4: "Serving Mammon." The *Star-Ledger* provided background material. Court transcripts, depositions, and formal complaints filed in court were invaluable, as were personal recollections.

Chapter 5: "Living a Life of Luxury." Articles by Courant.com and the *Darien Times* provided insight and general background information in this chapter. Court documents passed on a wealth of detail. Personal recollections were a very important source. The Diocese of Bridgeport turned down requests for information and photos.

Chapter 6: "Satan Takes a Bride." Articles published by

*Court Television News* and the *Blade* provided background information in this chapter. Primary sources were court records and personal recollections.